MARILEE PETERS

MAKING IT RIGHT

BUILDING PEACE, SETTLING CONFLICT

annick press
toronto + berkeley + vancouver

We acknowledge the support of the Canada Council for the Arts, the Ontario Arts Council, and the participation of the Government of Canada/la participation du gouvernement du Canada for our publishing activities.

 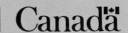

Funded by the Government of Canada

Financé par le gouvernement du Canada

CATALOGING IN PUBLICATION
Peters, Marilee, 1968–, author
    Making it right : building peace, settling conflict / Marilee Peters.

Includes bibliographical references and index.
Issued in print and electronic formats.
ISBN 978-1-55451-809-8 (paperback).—ISBN 978-1-55451-810-4
(hardback).—ISBN 978-1-55451-811-1 (html).—ISBN 978-1-55451-812-8 (pdf)

        1. Restorative justice—Juvenile literature. 2. Social justice—Juvenile
literature. 3. Criminal justice, Administration of—Juvenile literature. I. Title.

    HV8688.P48 2016   j364.68   C2016-900568-2
                                          C2016-900569-0

Distributed in Canada by University of Toronto Press.
Published in the U.S.A. by Annick Press (U.S.) Ltd.
Distributed in the U.S.A. by Publishers Group West.

Printed in China
Visit us at: **www.annickpress.com**
Visit Marilee Peters at: **www.marileepeters.ca**

Also available in e-book format.
Please visit www.annickpress.com/ebooks.html for more details. Or scan

TO MY KIDS, WHO TAUGHT ME A LOT
ABOUT FAIRNESS, EMPATHY,
AND FORGIVENESS—M.P.

TABLE OF CONTENTS

WHERE'S THE JUSTICE?

BREAK THE LAW—GO TO PRISON. Some people think justice is pretty black and white. What if there was another kind of justice? One that brought people together, healed them, and prevented crime?

"HEY, WE'VE BEEN RIPPED OFF!"

Your family arrives home at the end of the day to find the lock on the front door smashed. Inside, the place is a mess. You're standing in the doorway, knowing that strangers have been in your house, going through your things. Have they been in your room? What's missing? The TV, the computer, your mom's jewelry, the iPod you got for your birthday—all gone!

Later that night, after the police have gone and the mess has been tidied, you lie in bed trying to sleep. But you can't. You're tense with fear, flinching at every sound. What if the robbers come back? Will you ever feel safe in your own bed again?

Crime is a frightening reality around the world. In some countries, war, terrorism, and oppression are also parts of everyday existence—even for kids. Being caught up in a violent conflict is like a break-in that never ends. If you'd made it through a war—surviving bombings, shootings, and chaos—how do you think you would feel when the violence ended? Could you overcome your fear and anger and learn to live in peace with your former enemies?

Whether you've been a victim of crime or a victim of war, you've lost something precious: your trust in others. So is there a way to restore that trust and heal the damage caused by violence?

In our modern society, we typically deal with crime by sending the offender to prison. That keeps them from committing more crimes, at least for a while, and punishes them for breaking the law by taking away their freedom. But some people say that putting someone in jail isn't always the right solution—not for the criminal, and not for the people who were hurt by the crimes. Think about it: if your house had been broken into, what would you be more upset about—that the robbers had broken the law, or that they'd taken your belongings and made you feel unsafe in your own home? Most of us would probably give the second answer. Many people feel the same way after a war or conflict—they just want to live in peace again. And while locking away someone who has wronged you might satisfy your desire for revenge, would it really give you back that feeling of safety? What if there were a better way?

Imagine if there were no courtrooms, no lawyers, no judges or juries. Instead the victim, the offender, their families and maybe people from the community would sit down together with a facilitator and talk. They would talk about what happened, why it happened, and how it made them feel. Then they would talk about how to make things right.

WHETHER YOU'VE BEEN A VICTIM OF CRIME OR A VICTIM OF WAR, YOU'VE LOST SOMETHING PRECIOUS: YOUR TRUST IN OTHERS.

Does that sound like a fantasy? In fact, alternative ways of dealing with crime are already being used all around the world, maybe even where you live. Instead of focusing on punishment, they consider what victims, offenders, and communities need to heal rifts and repair damage. This kind of approach is often called **restorative justice**, and it's a different way of thinking about crime and its consequences.

Here's an example of how it works. One night, Lisa vandalized her local corner store and broke the window. She got caught. But Lisa was lucky: instead of going to court, the storeowner agreed to a restorative justice session. A few weeks later, a facilitator gathered Lisa, her parents, the storeowner, and some community members together to find a way to "make right" what Lisa had done. Lisa listened as the storeowner told them all how hard he had worked to open the store and how proud he was of it. She hung her head as he described how worried he got whenever teens came near the store now. Then Lisa explained that she and her friends were just bored and hanging out on the street corner, and that she threw the rock on a dare. She apologized to the storeowner.

After the group worked out a plan for Lisa to clean the store until she'd paid back the cost of a new window, they talked about ways to solve the problem of bored local teens—maybe they needed an after-school drop-in center. Instead of focusing on punishing Lisa, the group tried to figure out ways to make their neighborhood a better place.

When it works, this kind of approach helps victims heal, changes offenders' lives, and makes communities safer for everyone. Whether the issue is school bullies, vandals, war criminals, or oppressive governments, people are discovering that by working together they can look for solutions to conflicts and end violence. And guess what? There are lots of ways kids can get involved.

In this book, you'll find stories of young people from different parts of the world who are helping former enemies live together in peace. You'll delve into the history of justice to find out why we treat criminals the way we do and how different cultures throughout history have approached law and order. And you'll see how restorative justice can prevent conflicts, repair relationships, and cut down on crime and violence. If you still think this sounds too good to be true, remember: it's not a magic formula, but by working hard to listen and understand each other, people really can start to make the world a safer, more peaceful place.

Siobhan O'Reilly, George Carter, Heather Thurier, Lejla Hasandedic, Arn Chorn, and the other young activists you'll read about in these pages are real people. So are Russ Kelly, Frank Brown, and Michael Fay—young men who broke the law and got people thinking about whether our justice systems needed to be changed. To find their stories I read newspaper and magazine articles, researched them in books, and in some cases corresponded with them or spoke to them (or to people who had known them) by Skype. The short stories that open each chapter are fictional—but they are drawn from actual events, like the survey that Ugandan teenagers conducted to draw attention to the damage that the long war against the Lord's Resistance Army had caused. You can read about it in chapter six. I hope that story, and the others in this book, will give you ideas for things you can do to solve conflicts in your own life. If there's one thing I learned from all the amazing stories of brave young people I heard while writing this book, it's that every one of us can be a peacemaker—if we listen enough, understand enough, and care enough.

Chapter 1

JUSTICE 101

THINK RESTORATIVE JUSTICE IS NEW? Think again. Justice hasn't always been something that police, lawyers, and judges take care of for the rest of us. Throughout history, justice was settled one-on-one in most of the world. That's still the way it happens in some places.

PAPUA NEW GUINEA

Late one afternoon,

Mona and her little brother Pidi were walking through the village on their way home from school. As they neared their house, they could tell something was wrong: they heard shouts, thumps, and crashes. Then they noticed that the wooden fence around their family's garden was smashed. Mona and Pidi broke into a run. They raced up the path to their house. Their mother was on the porch, waving a stick and screaming at a herd of pigs that had broken into the garden and were trampling and rooting up the family's carefully tended vegetables.

Mona grabbed a rock. She took aim and threw it with all her force at the rooting pigs. *Whump!* The rock hit a big black-and-white sow in the back. The sow squealed and raced for a gap in the fence, just as Mona and Pidi's father appeared with his shotgun. He fired, and a pig dropped heavily to the ground. The rest of the marauding group disappeared through the broken fence, leaving Pidi, Mona, and their parents standing in the ruins of their garden.

Their father walked over to the dead pig and kicked it. "One pig," he growled. "Doesn't make up for what we've lost. There's nothing left in this garden. What will we eat now?"

"Where did all the pigs come from?" asked Mona. Many people in Papua New Guinea kept pigs, but this was a bigger herd than anyone in their village owned.

"I'll find out," their father answered grimly. "And they'll pay for this!"

He strode off toward the village, the gun over his shoulder. That evening, he returned with other men from the village. He showed them the damaged fence, the trampled garden, the dead pig that Mona and her mother were already butchering. The men talked seriously among themselves for a long time.

When everyone had left, Mona asked her father what was going to happen. "The pigs escaped from the next village," he explained. "Our neighbors will go there to tell them what their animals have done. The owner of those pigs owes our family sori money for this damage." In Tok Pisin, the language spoken in Papua New Guinea, *sori money* means "sorry money"—or money offered as compensation.

The next day, men from the nearby village arrived, bringing the owner of the runaway herd. The men from both villages sat down to discuss what was owed to Mona and Pidi's family. The owner pointed out he had lost one of his animals. Since Mona and Pidi's family had kept the pig they'd killed, he shouldn't have to pay as much.

"This family will have no harvest this year because your animals destroyed their garden," responded the headmen of the family's village sternly. "You must compensate them for that."

At last they reached an agreement, and the *tok sori* ceremony of apology began. The pig owner bowed low and apologized for the trouble his animals had caused. He promised to pay to repair the damaged fence, and to share vegetables from his garden to replace what the family had lost. Their father seemed satisfied, but Mona had a question.

"What if he doesn't pay the sori money?" she asked her father after everyone had gone. He looked at her seriously. "Then we must take revenge on him and his family. We must raid the village that has insulted us."

"WHAT IF HE DOESN'T PAY THE SORI MONEY?"

SHE ASKED HER FATHER.

"THEN WE MUST TAKE REVENGE ON HIM AND HIS FAMILY."

GUILTY OR INNOCENT?
IT'S A TOSS-UP

IN NORTH AMERICA, the Ojibwa people have a practice that teaches offenders—in a dramatic way—just how much they depend on their community. If someone has been causing harm to others, he might be placed on a blanket held by a number of men and tossed high in the air, over and over. Then, all at once, everyone lets go of the blanket and the offender lands with a thud on the ground.

Afterward, while he's nursing his bruises, the offender can think over what he's learned from the experience. As he was being tossed, higher and higher each time, he was very likely pleading with the group not to let go of the blanket. During those moments, as he waited for the bumpy landing he knew was ahead, it would have been clear to him just how much he needed the support of the others. The Ojibwa blanket toss shows offenders that the way to survive life's ups and downs is to develop and maintain good relationships with your community.

BACK TO THE BEGINNING

Throughout the long course of human history, we've tried many different ways to solve our conflicts. And we're still looking for the perfect solution: one that will hold offenders accountable, give victims justice, prevent more crimes from happening, and be fair to everyone.

In most parts of the world today, people live in countries with codes of laws that define what a crime is and how different crimes should be treated. When someone is caught breaking a law, they're arrested by the police and put on trial. If they're found guilty, they'll be punished. When the crime is serious, and especially if the person has committed other crimes before, they'll likely go to prison.

It takes a lot of people, money, and effort to make this system work: police, lawyers who argue for and against the accused person in court, judges who determine the sentence, prison guards, probation officers, social workers...the list goes on. In the United States, about 2.3 million people work in the criminal justice system. If you put all those people together in a city, it would be the fourth largest in the country.

PEOPLE WHO WORK IN THE CRIMINAL JUSTICE SYSTEM

8.5 MILLION

3.9 MILLION

2.7 MILLION

2.2 MILLION

2.3 MILLION

HOUSTON · CHICAGO · LOS ANGELES · NEW YORK

Governments put these justice systems in place to help keep the peace and protect their citizens, and many people now depend on them to help solve conflicts. Think about it. What would your family do if someone threatened you, hurt you, or stole your property? Many people's first reaction is to reach for their phone and call the police.

JUSTICE FOR ALL?

Modern justice systems in democratic countries are supposed to treat everyone equally—rich or poor, young or old, male or female, black or white. But it doesn't always work out that way. In many parts of America today, a black person who was the victim of a crime might think twice before calling the police for help. Police shootings, unfair arrests, and long prison terms have left many people—both black and white—feeling that the justice system is not there to help black people, but to hurt them. And the U.S. is not the only country where this kind of injustice happens. In many other countries, like Canada, Australia, and New Zealand, as well as in the U.S., indigenous peoples have been mistreated for hundreds of years, and have no reason to trust the police or the justice system.

IN MANY COUNTRIES, INDIGENOUS PEOPLE HAVE BEEN MISTREATED FOR HUNDREDS OF YEARS, AND HAVE NO REASON TO TRUST THE JUSTICE SYSTEM.

Now think about what you would do if there were no police—or lawyers, judges, or prison guards—in your community. What if it were up to you, your family, and your neighbors to solve all your problems and conflicts yourselves? How would you keep the peace in your community?

Until fairly recently, that's exactly what people in most societies have had to figure out. In some places, it's still the reality. The country of Papua New Guinea, near Australia, is a rough, mountainous island where many people live in small villages far from cities and modern police forces. Because there isn't a strong system of government, they continue to use the traditional justice practices that have existed for hundreds or even thousands of years.

Anthropologists (scientists who study human cultures) have studied how conflict is handled in Papua New Guinean villages. They've found that people in Papua New Guinea, like people living in other parts of the world where traditional justice is applied, think about conflicts quite differently from people who are used to having professionals handle their disagreements.

SORI MONEY...OR VENGEANCE!

In small traditional societies, there are usually two ways to solve a dispute: through negotiation and compensation, as happened with Mona and Pidi's family, or—if that fails—by violence. Mona's family received the compensation they felt they deserved. If they hadn't, people from her village would likely have gone to the other village to destroy or steal some of the pig owner's property. After that, the inhabitants of the other village might have felt they needed to take revenge, too. The dispute might have escalated into violence, even killing. A blood feud could go on for years, making life dangerous for everyone.

Luckily, in societies like Papua New Guinea's, everyone knows angry victims may seek vengeance after a crime has been committed. So people work hard to solve conflicts quickly, before more violence happens.

There are good reasons why many societies stopped using this kind of justice, though. For one thing, traditional justice systems aren't necessarily fair—in fact, they tend to favor powerful people. In many societies throughout the world, people have looked for ways to make their traditional systems fairer for everyone.

Traditional justice can work well for people who live in small villages or settlements. When you know everyone who lives around you, it's easy to see the importance of staying on good terms with your neighbors. With a little luck and a lot of hard work at maintaining peaceful relationships, your village can avoid getting drawn into a feud with another village. But what happens when your village grows into a city?

For city-dwellers, who may not know their neighbor, the traditional justice systems don't work as well. But with so many people living together, it's even more important to find ways to keep the peace in cities. Throughout history, in different societies around the world, as cities grew people realized they needed to do justice differently. Instead of leaving justice up to private citizens, city leaders decided to prevent blood feuds from starting by taking charge of delivering justice. Today, we call this "state justice." One of the first places where this is known to have happened was in the city-state of Babylon, near today's country of Iraq.

HAMMURABI PUTS IT IN WRITING

Nearly 4,000 years ago, a Babylonian ruler called King Hammurabi created one of the first written codes of laws. He had his royal stonecutters carve the laws (all 282 of them!) into a giant stone pillar, which he placed in the center of the city's marketplace where everyone would see it. Not many Babylonians could read, so most people wouldn't have known exactly what the laws were. But the massive black pillar, taller than a person on horseback, loomed over the marketplace as a daily reminder that the king made the laws, and the king would punish lawbreakers.

Under Hammurabi's code, offenders still paid compensation to their victims. The difference was, Hammurabi had decreed the amount of compensation for every kind of crime. And if an offender didn't pay up, he had to answer to Hammurabi and his soldiers—the victim didn't need to start a blood feud. The penalty for not paying could be harsh! Take Hammurabi's Law #8, for example:

> If a free man has stolen an ox or a sheep or an ass or a swine
> or a goat, if it is the property of a god or of a palace, he shall pay
> 30-fold; if it is the property of a serf, he shall replace it 10-fold. If
> the thief has not the means of payment, he shall be put to death.

For more than a thousand years, other cities and states based their systems of laws on Hammurabi's code.

DREADFUL DRACO

The ancient Greek civilization was one of the first to switch from the compensation system of justice to a system that punished wrongdoers. By the 7th century BCE, poor and middle-class citizens of Athens were protesting that the compensation system was unfair: when a rich person was killed, that person's family was paid a great deal of money. If a poor man or a slave was murdered, his family was entitled to much less. A leader named Draco promised to develop laws that would be fair to rich and poor alike. He made good on his word by replacing the traditional system of compensation with punishments.

Draco's laws were drastic. The punishment for murder? Death. The punishment for stealing fruit? Death. For sleeping in a public place? Death. The laws were so harsh, one Greek writer complained that Draco had written them in blood, not ink. So many people were being executed for minor crimes that there was soon even more unrest among the citizens of Athens. Luckily, after about 25 years of this *draconian* (yes, that word comes to us thanks to Draco) approach to lawmaking, the Athenians chose a new leader: a poet called Solon. By abolishing the death penalty for everything except murder and treason, and setting more reasonable punishments for minor offenses, Solon turned Athens's laws into a system that helped to build a stable, peaceful society. People were so grateful they started calling their new leader Solon the Lawgiver.

For hundreds of years, as cities rose and fell, citizens and rulers in China, India, and Rome struggled to write legal codes that punished wrongdoers, protected the innocent, and worked for the poor as well as the rich. But the next really big change in justice didn't come along until some 1,600 years after Solon's reforms.

THE PUNISHMENT FOR MURDER? DEATH.

THE PUNISHMENT FOR STEALING FRUIT?

DEATH.

FOR SLEEPING IN A PUBLIC PLACE? DEATH.

ALL HAIL THE CONQUEROR

In 1066 CE, an army from a northern region of France called Normandy invaded England and defeated the English. Today, we call this victory the Norman Conquest, and it was the start of tremendous changes in England. The leader of the French army, William the Conqueror, became the new king of England—although he didn't speak a word of English. William had a big job ahead of him: he needed to control the nation of unruly English people, and he needed to raise some money. Invasions, even back in 1066, were expensive, and the new king was short on cash.

William quickly realized that the legal system was one of the best tools he had for reminding his English subjects who was in charge now, and for filling his treasury. Under his direction, new laws were written, defining all crimes as an "offense against the king's peace." Because William was king, he was responsible for keeping the peace, and when a law was broken, William was the victim of that crime. It meant that now, if someone robbed you, they didn't have to pay *you* any compensation. Instead, they paid a fine to the *king*.

WHEN A LAW WAS BROKEN, KING WILLIAM WAS THE VICTIM. THE CRIMINAL DIDN'T HAVE TO PAY *YOU* ANY COMPENSATION. INSTEAD, THEY PAID A FINE TO THE *KING*.

William's innovation—making the state the victim in every crime—became the basis of modern criminal law systems across the world. And his new laws sparked other changes. Wealthy people who didn't want to pay the king's heavy fines started hiring lawyers to defend them in court. Other lawyers represented the king. The actual victims and offenders began to have less and less of a role in trials.

Of course, these changes didn't catch on overnight. In fact, for hundreds of years, English people, especially in the countryside, kept using traditional methods to solve small disputes. Families and village leaders decided who needed to pay what, to whom, depending on who had been injured or lost property. Gradually, though, justice in England was transforming into today's **retributive** system. Now, almost a thousand years later, modern criminal law systems all across the world are still based on William's big idea.

FROM PAYMENT...TO PUNISHMENT

Over the years, the English system of justice changed in other ways. At first, like Draco in Athens, the government tried to discourage criminals by demanding brutal punishments for many crimes. Criminals were whipped, beaten, locked into stocks and pillories, and, for serious crimes, executed. All these punishments took place in the public square, so everyone could see exactly what happened to those who dared to break the law. But instead of keeping the peace, the strategy seemed to create a crime wave: in the 16th century, during the 38-year reign of Henry VIII, there were 78,000 public hangings in Britain—nearly 40 a week!

By the 1800s, some people were starting to realize that executions and harsh punishments weren't working to prevent crime. Reformers began to argue that punishments should be more humane. So instead of ordering executions for minor crimes, judges began sending more criminals to prison. At first, conditions in prisons were so terrible that a prison sentence was really no different than a death sentence. Prisoners died of starvation, malnutrition, and "jail fever"—epidemics of disease spread through contaminated water and filthy conditions.

Beginning in the 19th century, prison reformers called for governments to clean up the jails, provide better food, and stop mistreating prisoners. The reformers hoped that if prisoners could survive jail, they might resolve to live better lives once they'd done their time. Slowly the idea grew that prisons shouldn't only punish people for doing wrong. They should also try to **rehabilitate** prisoners by giving them training and therapy so they wouldn't commit more crimes when their sentences were over.

As this idea caught on, prisons in a number of countries started offering education, training, counseling, and therapy so that when prisoners were released they could get jobs instead of going back to a life of crime. But those kinds of programs can be expensive, and not everyone agreed that they were working. There was still crime—lots of it—and some people argued that the way to stop it was to make the laws stricter and the punishments harsher. Starting in the 1980s, a "tough on crime" approach to justice became popular in the U.S., Canada, and many other countries. "Tough on crime" meant sending more people to jail, for longer sentences, even for small crimes. And "tough on crime" also meant cutting back on programs like education, counseling, and training.

The result? More and more people were going to prison every year. Lots of them were young people, and being in prison meant they missed out on finishing their education and getting job training. When they left prison, they had no skills, and with a prison record they had a hard time

IS THE JUSTICE SYSTEM KEEPING US SAFE?

OR IS IT ACTUALLY MAKING OUR COMMUNITIES MORE DANGEROUS?

finding work. That pushed them into crime again. This still happens in North America and many other parts of the world today. Chances are good that anyone who goes to prison once will end up there again and again.

It makes some people wonder: Is the justice system keeping us safe? Or is it actually making our communities more dangerous?

MODERN JUSTICE— TIME FOR A CHANGE?

Today, some people who study crime and justice believe we should bring back parts of traditional justice systems. Modern justice isn't working, they say. When someone commits a crime, they hurt real people in their community. But under our current justice system, offenders go to jail without having to face up to the harm they've caused. And victims? Their needs are mostly ignored by the court system. So more and more people who work with offenders and victims want to find constructive solutions to crime, and repair the relationships between the victim, the offender, and the whole community.

UNDER OUR CURRENT JUSTICE SYSTEM, OFFENDERS GO TO JAIL WITHOUT HAVING TO FACE UP TO THE HARM THEY'VE CAUSED.

Some people think that sounds like an "easy out" for offenders. "Where's the punishment?" they ask. In fact, when victims and offenders meet to work out their conflicts, it's very difficult for everyone—but especially for offenders. The victims may still be very angry. They usually ask tough questions, and then families and community members have their turn. Often, these meetings are filled with tears and shouting. Afterward, most offenders agree that going face-to-face with their victims is much harder than sitting through a court hearing—even harder than going to jail.

Does it work every time? Of course not. Sometimes victims don't want to participate—because they're too frightened, or too traumatized by the crime, or because they just want to forget what happened to them. Sometimes the offender isn't ready to accept responsibility for what he or she has done. But when the process goes well, the victims and the offenders leave with a new understanding of each other. Sometimes, restorative justice meetings end with hugs. In a few cases, victims and offenders have kept in touch after the meetings, and the victims have encouraged and supported the offenders as they try to rebuild their lives and stay out of trouble with the law.

This approach is a big change from the way most countries in the world now treat crime, and not everyone agrees it's a good change. Some people think strict laws and harsh punishments are needed to prevent crime. Ask these people for an example of a country where severe punishments seem to be working, and they might say, "What about Singapore?"

FAIR'S FAIR

DO PEOPLE HAVE an innate sense of justice? Some psychologists think so. Imagine if you'd been part of this famous research experiment: you're brought into a room and told to do a simple task—fold some towels or put some files in alphabetical order. The researchers tell you that they've matched you with a partner who is doing the same task in another room, and you'll both be paid afterward. In reality, though, there are no partners—the researchers made that up. When you're done, they tell you that your partner finished first, and they paid him $3. But don't worry—your partner has to share some of the money with you. He was given three choices for splitting the money: you could receive $1, $1.50, or $2. They hand you the money that your partner supposedly chose to share with you and, before you leave, the researchers ask you one final question: How do you feel about the amount you received?

It turned out that the people who participated in this experiment were happiest when their imaginary partner gave them $1.50, or exactly half the money. When they only received $1, they felt angry and cheated. But they weren't happy when they got $2, either—that was more than they felt they deserved. It didn't matter that the amount of money was very small—the subjects in the study wanted things to be fair.

The same principles apply to the way we think about crime and justice. Most people want punishments to be fair—not more than is reasonable for the crime, but enough that we feel justice has been done.

A CANING IN SINGAPORE

On May 5, 1994, 18-year-old Michael Fay became the first U.S. citizen in more than a century to be caned as punishment for a crime. Michael was living with his mother and stepfather in Singapore, a bustling city-state in Southeast Asia, when he got into trouble with the police. Singapore is famous for being a safe, clean city, and it has very strict laws against vandalism and destruction of public or private property. Singapore even has laws banning chewing gum!

Michael knew about the laws, but he wasn't thinking about them the night he and his friends ran wild in downtown Singapore, spray-painting parked cars, stealing traffic signs, and slashing car tires. Even when the police came knocking at Michael's door, asking questions about his part in the vandalism spree, he didn't realize how serious things were. He soon would.

A few months later, a Singapore judge found Michael guilty of having vandalized two cars with spray paint. For his crime, he was sentenced to four months in jail, a $2,230 USD fine—and six lashes with a bamboo cane. It was the lashing that got the media interested. Soon, Michael was a top news story around the world: the out-of-control American teenager who was going to be caned. There was so much uproar about the case that U.S. President Bill Clinton asked the Singapore government to reduce the sentence, and in the end Michael had to endure just four strokes of the cane, as well as the time in jail and a slightly lower fine.

When Michael was brought into the caning room, a doctor, the prison superintendent, and two prison officers were waiting for him. The doctor examined Michael to make sure he was fit to receive the punishment, then watched as his legs and hands were shackled to a wooden frame. An officer took a long bamboo rod, raised it high over his shoulders, and brought it down hard on Michael's buttocks. Once. Twice. Three times. Four.

Afterward, the doctor wiped away the blood and applied antiseptic to the wounds. The guards helped Michael limp back to his cell. The punishment had taken less than a minute, though the scars from a caning can last a lifetime.

Did Michael yell? Struggle? Cry? Plead for mercy? The records from Singapore's Queenstown Remand Centre don't tell us how the teenager reacted to his punishment. Some prisoners who are caned faint from the pain. It's safe to say no one who has been caned ever forgets it. But does it make them change their ways? Here's what happened to Michael after his minute in the caning room.

The next day Michael met with his lawyer. The reporters who were waiting outside the prison gates had one important question for his parents as they left: "Was Michael able to sit down?" The answer was yes. Michael was already healing from his injuries. But the punishment didn't keep him from continuing to break the law. Soon afterward, Michael left Singapore and returned to the United States. And just two years later he was back in trouble. In 1996, police in Florida arrested Michael and charged him with reckless driving, not reporting a crash, and having an open bottle of alcohol in his car. Two years later, he was arrested again: this time for possession of marijuana.

TO CANE OR NOT TO CANE?

Michael Fay's case attracted a lot of attention, especially in countries where physical punishments like caning aren't used against criminals anymore. For many people in North America, Europe, Australia, and other parts of the world, it came as a shock to learn that in a big, modern city like Singapore, criminals were still being punished this way. Many thought a beating seemed like excessive punishment for spraying graffiti.

Of course, not everyone opposed Michael's caning. In fact, newspapers were flooded with letters from people who supported Singapore's decision and complained about the amount of graffiti, vandalism, and crime in American cities.

CRIME AND JUSTICE AROUND THE WORLD

Being sentenced to a lashing seems like a punishment straight out of the history books. So does that mean that Singapore's justice system is old and outdated too?

Not necessarily. In fact, apart from the punishment, Michael's experience with the Singapore justice system was not all that different from what he would have experienced in the U.S. That's because these days justice systems in many parts of the world work the same way. It doesn't matter if you're in Paris, Pittsburgh, or Pretoria, if you're arrested for a crime, the process of deciding whether you're innocent or guilty will go something like this:

Imagine that, like Michael, you're out one night with a bunch of your friends. At first you're all just fooling around, but then your buddy pulls some spray cans out of his backpack. Soon, everyone is taking turns spray-painting cars, walls, and signs. A neighbor calls the police, and when you hear the sirens, you and your friends scatter, running for home.

As soon as the police arrive on the scene, they start investigating. They talk to witnesses and gather the evidence (empty paint cans, a dropped backpack, the baseball cap that flew off your head as you tore out of there). Before long, they've identified the suspects, and soon they're ringing your doorbell: you're under arrest for vandalism.

Next, the case goes to the prosecutor—a government lawyer whose job is to prove in court that you and your friends are guilty and deserve to be punished. The prosecutor will examine the evidence the police have collected, to make sure they can bring a strong case against you. If the lawyer feels there's enough evidence, your case will go to court. If you haven't already, now you'd better get a lawyer of your own. If you can't pay for a lawyer, some countries have legal aid systems that will appoint a lawyer for you. But many people feel that this is just one of the ways the current system is unjust—while the wealthy can afford their own lawyers, poorer people may have to depend on overworked public defenders.

After hearing your story and looking at the evidence, your lawyer will recommend that you plead either guilty or not guilty to the charges. Whichever way you plead, your lawyer will probably tell you not to talk to the people whose cars you damaged and advise you not to say you're sorry for what you did. That's because your lawyer's job is to make sure

WHILE THE WEALTHY CAN AFFORD THEIR OWN LAWYERS, POORER PEOPLE MAY HAVE TO

DEPEND ON

OVERWORKED

you aren't punished unfairly. Even if you plead guilty, your lawyer will argue that you shouldn't get a harsh penalty.

Once your case goes to court, lawyers argue about what happened while you sit listening quietly. Were laws broken? Can they prove who did it? You might be called to testify. You'll have to answer tough questions from the lawyer for the prosecution, who's trying to prove you guilty. A judge, and in some cases a jury, listens to the arguments on both sides and considers the evidence.

Finally, the judge or jury decide your fate. Are you innocent or guilty? Will you walk away free or are you going to spend time in a detention center or on probation? Your future is on the line!

Of course, there are differences in this process, depending on the laws in each country and how they are applied. But in most places in the world, when a law is broken, police, lawyers, and judges all have an important role to play in making sure that justice is done and the offender gets what he or she is seen to deserve.

Yet there's something missing in this description of a modern criminal trial. Can you spot it?

THE MISSING VICTIM

During your trial, you sat and listened to the lawyers' arguments, the witnesses' testimony, and to the judge or jury's decision. There may have been someone else in the courtroom listening just as hard as you: the victim. As the offender, you didn't have a say in what was going to happen to you. Neither did your victim.

When we read in the news that someone has been sent to prison, we might say, "Justice has been done." But has it really? While our law courts are often good at determining guilt or innocence, that doesn't mean they deliver justice for everyone. Sometimes crime victims leave the courtroom feeling as if they've been robbed a second time—cheated out of the chance to tell the offender how they feel.

COPS & ROBBERS—IT'S NO GAME

On TV, the life of a police officer looks exciting and dangerous. They investigate serious crimes, hunt for clues, chase down bad guys, and make arrests—all in less than an hour. In real life, police officers make arrests much more rarely: once a week or so for the average officer in North America. In fact, some researchers in New York found that in the 1980s, when crime rates were much higher than they are today, 40 percent of police officers didn't make a single **felony** arrest in a year. A felony is a serious crime, as opposed to a **misdemeanor**, or minor offense.

Police officers play an important role in keeping our communities safe, but they're not arresting murderers and thieves every day. What other mistaken impressions do we have? Well, for starters, what about our idea that justice systems treat everyone equally? In lots of places around the world—including the United States, Canada, and Australia— you're much more likely to get picked up by the police if you're poor, young, and not white. And when they're found guilty, people who are black or Aboriginal tend to get stiffer sentences than white people who are convicted of the same crimes.

Dozens of studies in England and the United States have shown that black men are far more likely to be stopped by police, and more likely to be arrested than men of other races. One of every three black men in the United States will go to prison during his life—and black teenagers who don't manage to finish high school have a better chance of going to prison than they do of getting a job. The situation is not much better for Americans from Hispanic families: one out of six Hispanic men in the U.S. will go to jail. White Americans face very different odds—only one in twenty-three white American men will end up in jail.

In Canada, Australia, and New Zealand, the numbers of Aboriginal people serving time are almost as shocking as the statistics for blacks in the U.S. Young Aboriginal people in Canada end up in jail 10 times more often than white Canadians. In Australia, one out of every seven Aboriginal people has spent time behind bars. And in New Zealand, half of the people in prison are Maori—even though Maori people make up just 15 percent of the total population.

IN THE U.S.

1 OUT OF 3 BLACK MEN WILL GO TO JAIL

1 OUT OF 6 HISPANIC MEN WILL GO TO JAIL

1 OUT OF 23 WHITE MEN WILL GO TO JAIL

Why do people from one group get arrested more often than people from another group? The answers are very complicated: race, poverty, education, and the history of the relationship between the groups are just some of the issues involved.

Could restorative justice approaches help solve racial inequalities and other problems in the current justice system? In restorative justice sessions, offenders have to answer tough questions, like "Why did you do this?" and "How were you feeling when you did it?" These questions push everyone to look deeply at the situations that push people toward violence and crime: things like poverty, racism, injustice. Sometimes a restorative justice meeting helps community members understand that by making changes in their neighborhood, their city, or even their country, they can help stop crime before it starts.

YOUTH JUSTICE IN SINGAPORE TODAY

If Michael Fay had committed his crime in 2014 instead of 1994, would he still have been caned? Maybe not.

In 2001, Singapore decided to try a new approach to youth crime. Now, when a young Singaporean gets into trouble with the law, a family conference is sometimes called. If the offender is ready to take responsibility for what they've done by admitting guilt, a family conference facilitator arranges a meeting between the offender and the victim. They come up with a plan for the young person to compensate the victim and make amends to the community.

There is still a regular trial in the courts, but before the judge decides on the sentence, he or she will read the plan from the family conference — and if the judge is satisfied with the plan, it becomes the sentence. The judge can also order additional measures, such as counseling, probation, or a curfew for the young person. Jail and caning are still possibilities. But as Singaporeans are discovering, when young people participate in restorative justice, the chances that they will commit another crime go down. In fact, since Singapore started using family conferences in the early 2000s, the crime rate in Singapore has been falling steadily. In 2014, it was at its lowest in 30 years.

LIVING NICELY TOGETHER

WHAT DO WORDS like "law" and "justice" mean to you? It's easy to forget that your culture's understanding of these concepts is just one way of looking at them—and that other cultures may have very different meanings for these words.

In Kanien'keha, the language of the Mohawk people of eastern Canada and the United States, there is no word for law. The word that translates most closely to "law" actually means "the way to live most nicely together."

Aboriginal justice systems in North America, Australia, and New Zealand placed emphasis on healing relationships after they had been damaged by crime or violence. Those traditions have had a big influence on the development of restorative justice today.

Chapter 2

BULLiES, BRAINS, & CHiMPS

YOU DON'T NEED to go to law school or join the police force to learn how to use justice for peace instead of punishment. Kids are using it to prevent bullying and make their schools and communities safer.

LONDON, ENGLAND

Sandy's mother popped her head in the door. "Dinner's in five minutes. Can you come and set the table, please?"

Thirteen-year-old Sandy was quiet through dinner, picking at the food on her plate. As her mother stood to gather the dishes, Sandy took a deep breath. "Mom, can I show you something? I don't know what to do." She pulled her phone from her back pocket.

Hours later, Sandy and her mother were still sitting at the table, scrolling through weeks of social media posts, tweets, and texts. "You're such a loser." "Everyone hates you." "Watch your back, bitch, we're going to get you." Sandy knew who was behind it all: her two former best friends.

Sandy's mother wanted to report the girls to the police, or at least call their parents. Sandy cried and begged her not to. "Mom, please just let me switch schools," she pleaded. Finally, they agreed: they would talk with a counselor at Sandy's school about the bullying.

The counselor had a suggestion: bring the girls together to discuss the problem and work out a solution.

The facilitator set some ground rules for the session, then got things going. "Irene, can you tell us how this began?" Irene began to explain the misunderstanding that had started everything, and how she and Crystal had decided to get revenge on their former friend.

The facilitator turned to Crystal. "How do you think what's happened has affected Sandy?"

Crystal looked startled. "I guess she feels mad at us? Maybe she wishes she hadn't been friends with us in the first place?"

The facilitator turned in his chair. "Sandy, it's your turn. Can you tell us how you feel about what's been happening? What's been the hardest part for you?"

"The worst," she said, "was every time I turned on my phone, I hoped you'd have texted me that it was over." Instead, there were more hateful posts. Sometimes, Sandy confessed, she thought about killing herself.

As she finished, Sandy noticed that Crystal and Irene were both crying. "We never meant for things to go this far," they said. Soon, they all agreed that Crystal and Irene would would go online to correct the lies they had spread about Sandy.

SHE KNEW WHO WAS BEHIND IT ALL: HER TWO FORMER BEST FRIENDS.

GETTING INSIDE THE BULLY BRAIN

Whether a bully tries to harm you in person or uses social media, it can be a terrifying experience. Some kids have been so tormented by bullying they've committed suicide to escape it. In schools around the world, parents, teachers, and kids are working to put an end to bullying.

As scientists learn more about the psychology of bullying, they're realizing that sometimes bullies don't fully understand how their actions are affecting others. Letting bullies hear directly from their victims how angry, scared, and lonely they feel can help to prevent these kids from going on to bully again. But what makes some kids bullies in the first place?

KILLERS OR KISSERS: CLUES TO HUMAN BEHAVIOR

In the 1970s, a **primatologist** (a scientist who studies nonhuman primates like chimpanzees, apes, and orangutans) named Frans B. M. de Waal spent six years studying a colony of captive chimpanzees in the Royal Burgers' Zoo in the Netherlands. He was interested in discovering whether the chimpanzees used aggression to become leaders within the group, so he paid close attention whenever fights broke out in the colony—and he kept careful track of what happened after the fight. Did the winner become more powerful in the colony? Was the loser shunned by the others afterward?

Primatologists look for connections between the way primates behave and our human society. They try to understand whether certain types of human behavior could have roots in our evolutionary past. At the time de Waal started his research, there was a popular theory that the leaders among primates were the most aggressive males. This was known as the "killer ape" theory, and it seemed to explain why humans harm others. According to the killer ape theory, violent primates were more successful: they lived longer, ate more, and fathered more babies. Violence had evolved as a survival strategy, the theory said, and humans were still following that strategy.

If the killer ape theory was correct, did it mean humans were preprogrammed to be violent? In fact, the longer de Waal watched the chimpanzees in their enclosure at the zoo, the more he realized co-operation was the most important characteristic of chimpanzee society.

Chimpanzees, like humans, are social animals, living in large groups. By cooperating with each other, they help ensure that their colony is successful and everyone survives.

One day, de Waal witnessed a vicious fight between two chimpanzees. A dominant male attacked another member of the colony, a smaller female. Other apes came to her defense. Soon screaming and chaos erupted among the group. For the rest of the day, the entire colony seemed upset—until, much to the scientist's surprise, the two warring apes suddenly wrapped their arms around each other! The other chimpanzees exploded in a chorus of hooting, as if celebrating that the disagreement had been settled. After that, life in the colony returned to normal.

Over the next several years, de Waal watched the same scenario happen again and again among the chimpanzees, until he had recorded hundreds of these "reconciliations." Almost every time chimpanzees fought with each other, they made up afterward. And when they didn't do it themselves, another chimpanzee—usually a family member of one of the fighters—would step in as a kind of mediator to help the reconciliation along, by hugging or grooming one of the former fighters before leading him over to his former enemy. The mediator would stay with the pair until they were calm.

By documenting that our primate relatives worked to solve conflicts, de Waal showed that peacemaking was part of our genetic inheritance before we evolved into humans.

De Waal's theories changed many people's thinking about both primates and humans. But they leave us with one big question. If solving conflicts is so easy for chimpanzees, why is it still so hard for humans?

ACCORDING TO THE KILLER APE THEORY, **VIOLENCE** HAD EVOLVED AS A SURVIVAL STRATEGY.

DID IT MEAN HUMANS WERE PREPROGRAMMED TO BE VIOLENT?

BORN TO DISAGREE?

We may not be killer apes, but humans aren't designed to get along with everybody all the time. We each have our own thoughts, our own opinions, and our own unique perspectives on the world. Those differences alone are enough to cause conflicts. Then throw in our different families and upbringings, cultures, political systems, and religions and it seems a miracle anyone can agree on anything!

Even within our own families and groups of friends, disagreements are common. In fact, one study found that teenagers reported having an average of eight conflicts every day. The most frequent disagreements were between kids and parents, or kids and their close friends or siblings.

Turning conflict into something positive might seem like an impossible goal, but it can happen. Back at the Royal Burgers' Zoo in the Netherlands, de Waal noticed that after fighting chimps made up, they seemed to spend more time near each other than they had before their conflict. But he wondered if he was simply paying extra attention to chimpanzees that had recently been fighting. So he began filming the colony. In the weeks following a fight, he would go over his films carefully, measuring the distance the two ex-fighters maintained, and comparing it to the distance between them in the days leading up to the fight. The data proved he was right. After fights, chimpanzees that had reconciled actually stayed closer to each other. Their relationships had improved.

> AFTER FIGHTS, CHIMPANZEES THAT HAD RECONCILED ACTUALLY STAYED CLOSER TO EACH OTHER. THEIR RELATIONSHIPS HAD IMPROVED.

ENDING CONFLICT WITH EMPATHY

In human societies, one of the keys to resolving conflicts is **empathy**—our ability to understand other people's feelings. Imagine you're out walking with a friend when suddenly she trips and falls, skinning her knees on the sidewalk. "Ouch!" you yell—as if it were *you* who'd had the accident.

You're reacting with empathy, and it's the way nearly everyone responds to seeing people hurt themselves. It's almost as though we can actually feel someone else's pain. Empathy is automatic for most people, but it is actually a pretty complex response. To explain how it works, de Waal developed a theory he calls the Russian Doll Model.

Picture a Russian doll, the kind you can pull apart to find smaller dolls inside. This Russian doll has three layers: there's an outer doll, with a smaller doll inside, and inside that an even smaller doll. The smallest doll is our deepest, most primitive layer of empathy, and we share it with almost all mammals. It's what helps us react so quickly when we see someone who's hurt or upset. Without even thinking about it, we *know* how he or she must feel.

The middle doll is the layer where we start *thinking* about how someone must feel—it's a more complicated reaction, in which we actively try to understand what the other person might be feeling ("Her knees probably really sting!"). At the layer of the biggest doll, we start *doing* something for the other person. We're able to assume their perspective to see what they need and how we can help ("I'll take her home so she can wash those cuts.").

When you're fighting with someone, feeling empathy can be tough. Acknowledging another perspective means letting go of "being right."

THE SMALLEST DOLL IS OUR

DEEPEST,
MOST
PRIMITIVE

LAYER OF EMPATHY,
AND WE SHARE IT WITH ALMOST
ALL MAMMALS.

You might have to recognize that you were wrong, or that you hurt the other person. That's why in most traditional justice systems, other people in the community step in to help with negotiations after someone has been harmed.

Kids aren't usually involved in working out solutions for conflict. Generally, in smaller, traditional societies, people take their disagreements to village elders. Because the elders are well-respected and powerful, they can persuade everyone to agree with their decisions. In state justice systems, where crimes are handled by the police and the courts, there's no role for kids either.

Even when conflicts occur between kids, it is often adults who resolve the situation. In schools, teachers and principals are usually the ones to step in and take charge when kids fight, doling out punishments like detentions and suspensions—even expelling kids if they've caused trouble too often. Some teachers have started to question this approach, though. They're asking, "How does this prepare young people to take on the responsibility for solving conflicts as adults?"

Many people now believe that empathy is like a muscle: the more you use it, the stronger it grows. In more and more schools around the world, kids are learning how to use their natural empathy to listen to others, stop fights, and find peaceful solutions to disagreements. In fact, kids as young as five can help each other solve disagreements—without having to call for assistance.

When schools make the switch from regular discipline, in which teachers use punishment to solve problems, to an approach that says, "You've done a bad thing; let's find a way to make it better," it helps kids to understand the person they've hurt, as well as themselves.

THE MUSIC OF EMPATHY

DANIEL REISEL IS A NEUROSCIENTIST, someone who studies how the brain affects behavior. In 2001, he wanted to understand why some people seemed unable to feel empathy. Reisel ventured into the Wormwood Scrubs Prison in London, to ask England's most dangerous men if he could study their brains.

Scientists believe that empathy is controlled by the **amygdala,** a cluster of cells deep in the brain. When the prisoners were shown a picture of someone looking tearful, they could tell the person was sad, but their amygdalas didn't respond normally. "It was as though they knew the words, but not the music of empathy," Reisel says.

Did this mean violent criminals were hardwired to be psychopaths? Not if their brains could change, Reisel decided. But most people assumed adult brains couldn't grow new brain cells. Could they?

To answer these questions, Reisel began working with some very different research subjects: mice. Mice brought up in isolation develop strange, violent behaviors. When Reisel put them into contact with other mice, their behavior gradually changed—because their brains grew new cells.

Reisel now believes that adult humans can learn empathy too. And the best way for them to do that? From the very people they've hurt. When criminals face their victims and take responsibility for their actions, Reisel thinks, it stimulates their amygdalas to grow new brain cells that help them change their behavior. That's why Reisel is now training to become a restorative justice facilitator—to find a way for violent criminals to learn to develop empathy.

CHAMPIONS OF EMPATHY

Students at the Downtown Alternative School in Toronto were some of
the first in North America to learn how to settle their disagreements
and solve their problems on their own. In the 1980s, a filmmaker named
Roberta King visited the school and filmed kindergarten students on the
playground as they used the peacemaking techniques they'd learned.
Over the next 14 years, she went back and interviewed those students
as they grew up, to find out whether what they'd learned about solving
disputes was helping them in their lives.

When kids at the Downtown Alternative School couldn't agree, they
would ask two other children who weren't involved in the fight to be the
peacemakers. The peacemakers would lead everyone to a quiet spot: out
into the hallway if they were in the classroom, or to a private corner of
the playground if they were outside. Everyone sat down in a circle, and
the peacemakers started by asking a series of questions.

> *Do you both agree to solve the problem?*
>
> *Do you agree to let the other person talk without interrupting?*
>
> *Do you agree to no name-calling or insults?*
>
> *Do you agree to tell the truth?*

Sometimes kids added new questions to this list when problems
came up in the peacemaking process—things like: *Do you agree to no
plugging your ears?* and *Do you agree to no touching?*

Once everyone had agreed to the ground rules, the peacemakers
would ask someone from each side to talk about what had happened
and how it made them feel. Often, as they listened to the two sides of the
story, it became clear to everyone why the fight had broken out. Usually,
it was a simple misunderstanding that had gotten out of hand.

After everyone had had a chance to talk, the peacemakers would ask, "What do you think is a good solution?" Again, the kids took turns, this time suggesting what could be done to solve the problem and prevent it from happening again. Sometimes the answers were obvious, but occasionally the peacemakers had to work hard to find a solution everyone agreed was fair.

If you think the Downtown Alternative School's peacemaking methods sound familiar, you're right. The techniques these young kids were using to solve problems on the playground had been working for thousands of years in traditional societies around the world. The students interviewed by King years later all talked about how the Downtown Alternative School had felt like a big family, where everyone was accepted for who they were. And by solving their conflicts themselves, no one got sent to the principal's office!

The kids King talked with as teenagers laughed as they thought back on the fights they'd had in kindergarten over taking turns on the tire swing or getting glitter on another child's art project—and they remembered working hard to solve those disagreements.

The key to the success of the peacemaking program? Listening. By taking the time to listen carefully without interrupting, the peacemakers heard everyone's version of events, and they were able to help the kids involved to understand the other side's point of view. One boy remembered being a peacemaker as "really exciting—you swoop in to where kids are fighting and help solve the fight." But unlike a superhero who flies in, rescues someone, and flies off again, part of what makes peacemakers so powerful is that they are sharing their powers—every time they help solve a conflict, some of their peace-building skills rub off on others.

USING YOUR SUPERPOWERS FOR GOOD

IF YOU HAD SUPERPOWERS, would you use them for good or evil? According to a study at California's Stanford University, being a super-hero—even temporarily—makes us more likely to be helpful in real life.

Using a virtual reality lab, people in the study strapped on goggles that transported them to a digital cityscape where they were given a mission: they needed to rescue a small child stranded somewhere in the city. In this virtual world, some of the participants could fly like Superman. Others had to take a helicopter to find the child.

Afterward, when they'd taken off their goggles and returned to reality, the participants were given an opportunity to help someone in real life. The researchers found that the people who'd had the ability to fly were more helpful than the ones who'd flown in the helicopter. Turns out that feeling as though we have the power to make a difference makes us more likely to help others.

PEACEMAKING IN BRAZIL

In 1999, a young Englishman named Dominic Barter moved to the Brazilian city of Rio de Janeiro. He lived near one of that city's largest *favelas*, or shantytowns. The favela, built on the steep hills outside Rio, is a maze of twisting, narrow roads lined with tiny houses. The people are poor, and life in the favela is hard: some homes don't have running water or dependable electricity.

Life there is also dangerous. When Dominic arrived in Rio, criminal gangs controlled the favelas. Kids as young as seven and eight delivered drugs for the gangs. Arguments were solved with guns. Murders and shootings happened every day. Dominic was scared, but he wanted to help his neighbors solve their problems without violence. He figured if people could find peaceful ways to settle disputes, they'd be able to take back control of their community from the gangs. So he began spending time talking with residents, learning how the violence in the favelas had started, and why.

As people learned to trust Dominic, they began asking for his help to solve disputes. So Dominic organized meetings that brought together victims, offenders, family members, and people from the community. Dominic's idea was that since violence was a community problem, the community needed to be part of the solution.

At first, some people were afraid to take part in Dominic's meetings. They worried they'd become targets for gang members looking for revenge. But as people realized that this method of talking through problems was cutting down the violence on their streets, the meetings became more and more popular. Eventually, Dominic decided to give them a name. He called them restorative circles. Soon his circles were being used to help resolve everything from arguments between husbands and wives to murders committed by rival gangs. Then Dominic realized the circles could solve disputes among kids as well as adults. He trained teachers to lead circles in the favelas' schools. At first, they were very popular, but after a while, the teachers told Dominic that their

STUDENTS HAD STOPPED ASKING TEACHERS TO CONDUCT THE MEETINGS.

THEY WERE ORGANIZING THEIR OWN CIRCLES.

students had stopped asking them to conduct the meetings. Puzzled, Dominic visited the schools—and discovered that students were organizing their own circles. The kids had absorbed and adapted the process, making it their own.

Today, restorative circles have spread from Rio's favelas to cities and towns all around Brazil. Has violence in the favelas disappeared? Sadly, no. They are still dangerous places to live. But thanks to the circles, more young people are realizing that guns and violence aren't the only ways to solve disagreements. Slowly, life in the favelas is changing.

BEYOND BULLYING: SOLVING INJUSTICE AT SCHOOL

Sometimes, the problems kids have at school aren't with other students, but with the school itself. That's the situation George Carter and other black students in the city of New Orleans faced after a hurricane damaged many of the city's schools in 2005.

George was just seven years old when Hurricane Katrina tore through his city. His school was closed for months afterward, and when it finally reopened conditions were bad. The toilets didn't work properly, and there weren't enough books to go around, or enough chairs for everyone. There weren't even knives and forks. It was the same in many public schools in New Orleans's poorest neighborhoods.

George, and other kids like him, figured that students should have a voice in improving their schools. To get their ideas heard, they formed a group called Kids Rethink New Orleans Schools, or the Rethinkers for short. They may have been kids, but the Rethinkers' ideas weren't childish. Each year they focused on one big problem, finding creative solutions and then working to get their changes into schools. The first year, they took on "bathroom reform," convincing the school board to renovate 350 broken school bathrooms. Then they turned their attention to getting healthy food served in school cafeterias and building school gardens.

But there was still one big barrier to success for lots of New Orleans students: the "school-to-prison pipeline." Researchers in the United States had noticed that kids who were suspended from school, even once, were more likely to get into trouble with the law than other students, and were also more likely to drop out or be expelled—which made their chances of going to jail even higher. Researchers also found that black students were kicked out of school three times as often as white students. The suspensions were sending those kids a message: "You don't belong in school."

The neighborhoods where kids who didn't finish high school lived were filled with crime, drugs, and gang violence. So in 2010 the Rethinkers decided to tackle the problem by advocating that schools replace suspensions with restorative justice. To make sure their ideas got attention, they held a press conference.

The Rethinkers took turns speaking to the press. When George came to the podium, he was so short that he could hardly reach the microphone. He suggested that schools should take down the metal detectors at the front doors that scanned kids each morning for weapons, and replace them with "mood detectors." He was joking, but there was a serious point behind the joke: when schools treated kids like criminals, with metal detectors and armed guards in the halls, the kids were more likely to behave like criminals. The Rethinkers wanted to see student peacemakers replace the guards.

The changes the Rethinkers proposed to bring peace to their schools have worked. At one of the first schools to introduce the new approach, the violent crime rate dropped by 64 percent.

But change doesn't always come fast enough. In 2014, when he was only 15 years old, George was shot and killed on a street near his home. His murder hasn't been solved.

A few months before he was killed, George made a speech about reforming schools. He said, "I believe that the solution is in us, the youth. We are the ones that can change our schools. We are the ones that go to the schools every day. We are the experts." The other Rethinkers are working harder than ever to change their schools and make life safer for all students.

BLACK STUDENTS WERE KICKED OUT OF SCHOOL THREE TIMES AS OFTEN AS WHITE STUDENTS. THE MESSAGE: "YOU DON'T BELONG IN SCHOOL."

BUILDING BRIDGES OF PEACE

Building peace doesn't have to stop at the school door. Just ask Lejla Hasandedic. Lejla is from Bosnia and Herzegovina, a country in south-eastern Europe that is still rebuilding after a vicious civil war in the 1990s between the Croats and the Bosniaks who lived there.

BEYOND THE LUNCH TABLE

WHEN EBOO PATEL was a high school student in Chicago, his friends were kids from many different countries and religious backgrounds— American, Nigerian, Cuban, Hindu, Christian, Muslim, and Jewish. Eboo's family were Ismaili Muslims who had come from India. Every lunch hour, Eboo and his friends sat in the cafeteria, discussing sports, girls, and movies. But they never spoke about their cultures or their religions.

When someone at the school scrawled anti-Semitic graffiti on their Jewish friend's locker, the boys didn't talk about that, either. When kids yelled hateful things at him in the hallways, they didn't know how to stop it, or what to do. So they pretended it wasn't happening, and because it made them uncomfortable, they avoided their friend.

Years later, in university, Eboo ran into his Jewish friend again. For the first time, his friend explained how he'd felt back then: frightened and friendless. Eboo realized that by pretending nothing was wrong, he had let his friend down. He decided that from then on he was going to speak up against intolerance.

Eboo went on to start a movement—the Interfaith Youth Core—to bring young people of different religious traditions together to learn about each other. Eboo says that his movement is especially important because young people are increasingly targeted and recruited by religious extremists and taught to hate people from other faiths.

On university and college campuses in the United States and other countries, Interfaith Youth Core groups help people understand what they have in common with those from other religions. By connecting with each other, Eboo hopes, we can stop hate from spreading.

In 1992, when she was just four years old, Lejla and her family escaped on the last bus from the besieged city of Sarajevo. They fled to the ancient city of Mostar, famous for its beautiful bridge over the Neretva River. Called the Stari Most, the bridge was built in the 16th century to connect the historic Turkish section of Mostar to the European part of the old city. Since its earliest beginnings, Mostar had been a multicultural city, where Muslims, Christians, and Jews lived together. But in 1992, Mostar was divided by the war. Soon, a bomb destroyed the bridge, and young Lejla, living in basements and moving from shelter to shelter with her family to hide from the constant gunfire and shelling, didn't even know it had once existed.

It wasn't until four years later, when the war had ended and Lejla was able to go to school, that she learned the history of the city she now called home. Almost everywhere in Bosnia and Herzegovina, Croats and Bosniaks were sent to separate schools, but Lejla was lucky: she attended an experimental school that accepted students from both groups. Even at Lejla's school, however, the Croatian and Bosnian children were kept apart—in separate classes, with different teachers and schedules—so although they shared the same building, they rarely saw each other. Lejla knew that things hadn't always been like this in Mostar, and she wondered about the Croatian children. Were they so different?

On her way home from school one day, Lejla noticed an unfamiliar girl, and introduced herself. In just a few minutes, the girls found out they both liked Barbies, makeup, and pop music—yet Lejla's new friend was Croatian. Lejla never forgot that girl, like her in so many ways. She became a member of a joint student council that brought together students from both parts of her school. The students talked about how

CROATIAN AND BOSNIAN CHILDREN WERE KEPT APART AND RARELY SAW EACH OTHER.

they could build connections between Croats and Bosniaks, and soon someone brought up the Stari Most. The bridge had been rebuilt after the war and was a popular attraction for tourists from around the world. But it was located in a Bosnian neighborhood, so most of the Croatian students had never even seen their city's most famous sight. The student council decided to change that.

It took a year of talking to convince the Croatian students that it would be safe, but finally, —together—the Bosnian and Croatian kids crossed the Stari Most to show they could break down the barriers dividing people in their city.

Today, almost 20 years later, Croats are no longer afraid to cross the Stari Most, and people live and work wherever they want in Mostar, regardless of whether they are Bosniak or Croats. Lejla is now a peace activist, still helping to build bridges between people in her country.

Chapter 3

YOUNG AND IN TROUBLE

WHEN SOMEONE HURTS YOU, you might want to try to get even, or you could look for solutions that will help you feel safe again. It takes skill and determination to choose the second path.

LEUVEN, BELGIUM

Dimi and Karsten were talking and laughing as they tramped homeward one warm summer night after seeing a movie. The two friends were both 18. They'd finished high school and were enjoying their holidays before heading to university in the fall.

As they crossed a street, a convenience store's neon sign caught Karsten's eye. "Let's grab a snack," he suggested. Dimi agreed.

Outside the store, a group of boys was hanging out, yelling to each other over the sound of music pumping out of a car stereo. Dimi and Karsten brushed by them and headed inside.

When they came out again, Karsten noticed the gang had moved down the street, clustered around a parked car. "Hey, I think those guys are trying to break into that car," he told Dimi. Without waiting for his friend, Karsten ran down the street, yelling at the gang to leave the car alone.

The next thing Karsten knew, the gang members had surrounded him, and begun pushing him back and forth. As one boy shoved him forward, another boy punched Karsten in the face. Reeling from the blow, Karsten lost his balance and fell backward, slamming his head against the curb. He blacked out instantly.

Karsten didn't wake up for two weeks. When he finally opened his eyes again, he was in intensive care. Instead of going to university that fall, Karsten stayed in the hospital for months, recovering from his brain injury.

When he was allowed home, there was a letter waiting for him from the Belgian court system. Did he want to take part in a Restorative Group Discussion? If he agreed, he would meet with the boy who'd hit him to see if they could agree on an alternative to a jail sentence. Angrily,

Karsten tossed the letter in the trash. As if he'd consider anything that would reduce that guy's sentence! He wanted his attacker to suffer, just like he'd suffered for months lying in a hospital bed. But as Karsten thought it over, he worried. Maybe someday another person would get hurt because Karsten hadn't made his attacker face up to what he'd done. Eventually, he agreed to the meeting.

When the other boy filed in, Karsten barely recognized him. The leering gang member he'd been picturing in his memory for months was actually a kid, younger than Karsten. Adrian was skinny and scared, kept his eyes on the ground, and barely mumbled hello to the facilitator.

The facilitator directed them to sit facing each other, and she asked Karsten to start by telling his story. Then he had a chance to ask Adrian the question that had been on his mind for months. "Why did you hit me?" he demanded.

The boy's head sagged. "You made us mad, I guess," he said softly. "It wasn't any of your business what we were doing. I thought you were a goody-goody for trying to stop us."

After hours of talking, Adrian and his parents stepped into another room to discuss how the boy could make amends. Adrian shuffled out with his head bowed, his face hidden deep in his hoodie. But when they returned, he seemed stronger, more self-assured. Adrian spoke clearly as he outlined what he could do: take an anger management course, volunteer with a group that helped victims of brain injuries, find a job to help Karsten pay for the costs of his rehabilitation therapies. For the first time, he looked Karsten in the eye. "I can't undo what happened. But I can make sure it doesn't happen again."

Karsten and his family agreed to the proposal. Karsten felt as though the air had been cleared. He hoped Adrian would change his life.

"I CAN'T UNDO WHAT HAPPENED. BUT I CAN MAKE SURE IT DOESN'T HAPPEN AGAIN."

PUNISH OR PREVENT?

If you've ever been really scared or angry, you know that it can be hard to think clearly. Just as people in extreme situations may make irrational decisions—wandering farther away from safety, for example—people who commit crimes sometimes can't explain why they decided to break the law. But they have to live with the consequences—including the possibility they will go to jail.

Criminologists (people who study criminal behavior), police, and politicians around the world have argued for years about whether longer, tougher sentences for criminals prevent people from committing crimes.

ONE FACT THAT NO ONE CAN ARGUE: ONCE YOU'VE BEEN TO JAIL, THE CHANCES ARE HIGH THAT YOU'LL GO BACK.

But there's one fact that no one can argue about: once you've been to jail, the chances are high that you'll go back.

People coming out of prison have trouble finding and keeping jobs. They may have trouble finding a place to live. Their relationships with their families and friends are often damaged from having been away for a long period of time. Above all, they feel as if they've been branded as criminals. That may be one of the biggest reasons people who have been in jail once commit crimes again.

RAISING HELL

Although restorative justice has its roots in traditional justice systems from all around the world, it wasn't an option for victims or offenders in most of the developed world until quite recently. Then something happened to change that. It's called the Elmira Case, and it all started one night in a small town in Ontario, in 1974.

Russ Kelly was 18, drunk, and mad as hell. It was nearly midnight on a warm May night, and Russ and a buddy had been driving the dark backroads around the little town of Elmira. They'd been having a good time: the radio was cranked up, and an open case of beer sat on the back seat. Russ was squealing his tires around the corners, tossing the empties out the window, when suddenly he saw a red, flashing reminder of everything he hated. It was the police, signaling them to pull over.

The cop poured their beers out and ordered the two boys to head for home. Russ knew they were lucky not to have been arrested for drinking and driving. But when he was drunk, he got angry, and Russ was furious at the police. He wasn't going to listen to them, just like he hadn't listened when his older brother had tried to run his life for him, after he took Russ in at age 15 following their mother's death. Russ could take care of himself. Hadn't he been doing it since he was seven years old, when his dad died? Russ turned the car toward town.

As they drove, Russ's friend suggested that instead of going home, they should "raise some hell." "Yeah," Russ said. "Why the hell not?"

FSSSSHHHH! Air hissed out of the slash from Russ's switchblade. Russ grunted with effort and yanked the knife out of the thick rubber. Twenty-two slashed tires later, his arm was aching and he was ready for something different. He tried the door of a car: unlocked! Russ reached in and ripped his knife across the driver's seat, shredding the fabric. He did the same to the passenger seat, then looked up to see his buddy dragging a picnic table out of a backyard. Russ ran to grab one end. Together, they hauled the table down the street and launched it into an ornamental pond, hooting at the sight of the table legs jutting crookedly out of the shallow water.

When a light came on in a bedroom window, they took off running. A few blocks later, Russ realized they were standing in front of the liquor store. Before he knew it, he had a rock in his hand. A second later, the rock was flying toward the store's plate-glass window. *CRASHHHH!* The sound of the glass shattering was so satisfying that soon both boys were scrabbling for more rocks, aiming them as they ran through town at car windshields, doors, traffic lights, more windows, even the glass display case in front of the town's church.

Russ's buddy reached through the shards of broken glass of the shattered display case and brought out a wooden cross. Grinning, he snapped the cross in pieces and tossed the fragments on the ground. Russ stared up at the sky, and noticed it was getting light. The anger and adrenaline that had kept him going suddenly drained away. He felt tired and confused. Why had they started this rampage? The two turned toward home, exhausted.

It was still early when the pounding began. When Russ realized the noise was coming from the front door, he pulled himself up, staggered toward the hallway, and yanked the door open. In the bright morning light that was flooding in, he could only see the outlines of the police officers' broad shoulders, but he recognized the snap of the handcuffs on his wrists: he was in trouble again. Big trouble.

TRYING NEW THINGS

Mark Yantzi was a young probation officer in Kitchener, Ontario, the city nearest Elmira. Every couple of weeks, he got together with a group of friends who also worked with kids in trouble with the law. Sharing his frustrations and ideas with the group helped to keep Mark going.

Mark was planning to meet with the group the day Russ Kelly's file landed on his desk. He felt so discouraged as he leafed through the report that he thought he might skip the meeting. Here was another example of a couple of dumb kids who were probably going to go to jail. He read about Russ's tough childhood and thought about what the future held for him. What could Mark do—what could anyone do—to change the direction this kid's life was headed?

Mark decided he needed to talk it out with his friends.

Everyone in Mark's group agreed that jail wasn't the answer. But what would help them and still be fair to the victims? Suddenly, Mark heard himself say, "Wouldn't it be neat for these offenders to meet the victims?" Around the table, heads were nodding. The group began putting together a plan to get Mark's ideas in front of the judge who would hear Russ's case.

When Judge McConnell first read Mark's proposal, he snorted, "It can't be done." Mark had suggested the two boys be put on probation on the condition they agreed to meet their victims, apologize to them, and pay them back for any damage that wasn't covered by insurance. There was no legal precedent for this kind of order—nothing in the law that would support the judge to make this decision.

Then Judge McConnell thought about the young people who came into his court over and over again, unable to pull themselves out of a cycle of crime and prison. The judge decided to take a chance on Mark's idea.

A YOUTH CHAMPION

HEATHER THURIER could see that the criminal justice system in Edmonton, Alberta, wasn't giving kids a fair break, and she had an idea to fix it. Heather was a 15-year old First Nations girl. In her short life, she'd been homeless, drug addicted, and in trouble with police. She knew what kids like her needed to get their lives on track: support. So she asked the local juvenile court if she and her friends could help other kids in trouble.

In 2001, the Youth Restorative Action Project was born. To help kids charged with crimes overcome homelessness, addiction, or mental health challenges, a member of YRAP would arrange a meeting with the youth and people affected by their crime. They'd draw up a contract, setting out everything the young person agreed to do to make up for the harm they'd done. Then YRAP supported each kid to work through their list.

Heather was YRAP's leader—even though when the project began, she was still homeless. For the first few months, Heather fed coins into a bus station locker each night and stuffed the YRAP files inside for safekeeping. It was a rocky start, but just three years later YRAP won a national award for its innovative approach to youth justice. The program is still going strong today, and programs like it have started up across Canada and the U.S. Tragically, Heather's story doesn't have a happy ending. In 2010, she was shot and killed by a 21-year-old gang member when she asked him for a cigarette. Heather's killer was the kind of troubled youth she'd spent years trying to help.

TAKING A CHANCE

When Mark explained his proposal to the two boys, their immediate answer was, "No way!" They were scared at the idea of facing all the people whose houses and cars they'd damaged. They'd rather go to jail. But once Russ thought it over, he wondered how else they could keep living in Elmira. Eventually, Russ convinced his friend to go along with the alternative sentence.

The first house was the worst. The door opened, and a small woman in slippers appeared, staring suspiciously at the boys. For a minute, everyone was silent. Then Russ introduced himself as the kid who'd broken her windows. It was hard to look her in the eye as he spoke. And he had to do it over and over again that day.

For hours the two boys trudged through town, up one block and down the next, listening to people's fear and anger. A white-haired lady with a "For Sale" sign on her lawn told them that since the night they'd put a rock through her front window, she'd been too frightened to stay alone in her house. Now, her family had decided it was time for her to move to a retirement home. As Russ listened, he thought, "She looks like my grandmother." As they left each doorstep, Russ and his friend promised to return and pay for what they'd done. Behind them, Mark scribbled notes, recording the money they owed.

The homeowners might not have expected to see the boys again, but three months later they were back, walking from house to house with certified checks. Russ had gone to work as a welder so he could pay back what he owed. With his welding tools, Russ had even made a new cross for the church's display case.

After that, Russ mostly stayed out of trouble, but his life wasn't easy. For years he kept abusing drugs and alcohol, trying to dull the pain of losing his parents. Then more bad luck struck Russ: he hurt his back so badly he couldn't work as a welder anymore. He needed new skills, so he decided to go to college.

One day, a speaker from an organization called Community Justice Initiatives visited his college law class to talk about a new way to keep young offenders out of jail: restorative justice. The speaker told the class about a famous case that had started it all, more than 20 years earlier. He called it the "Elmira Case." As he spoke, waves of shock rolled over Russ. When the class ended, he made his way to the front of the classroom and introduced himself to the speaker. "I'm Russ Kelly," he said. "You've been talking about me."

Russ ended up volunteering for Community Justice Initiatives and became a restorative justice mediator. And he shared his story, visiting high schools, colleges, churches, and prisons to talk about that night in Elmira, and how Mark Yantzi's idea had turned his life around.

IT WAS HARD TO LOOK HER IN THE EYE AS HE SPOKE. AND HE HAD TO DO IT OVER AND OVER AGAIN THAT DAY.

What if Mark hadn't suggested that Russ face his victims? What if Judge McConnell had decided the new idea was too risky? "It's scary even to think about that," says Russ today. "If I had gone to jail, I know I'd have come out a much worse person. I'd feel worthless and as though the world was against me."

WHAT'S THE BIG DIFFERENCE?

The difference between restorative justice and the regular court system comes down to a few simple points.

When police, lawyers, and a judge take a case through the court system, they're trying to answer three big questions:

Which laws were broken?

Who did it?

What punishment do they deserve?

When a restorative justice facilitator sits down with an offender, the person they've hurt, and family members, friends, and community members, they all look for answers to a different set of questions. The facilitator asks people to talk about:

Who was hurt?

What needs to happen to repair the harm?

Whose responsibility is it to see that the harm is repaired?

Some of the things victims of crime want are:

～ A restored feeling of safety

～ An explanation and answers to their questions

～ A chance to tell their story

～ Something to put things back in balance: an apology, for example, or compensation from the offender

People hurt by a crime may ask:

Why did you do it?

Why did it happen to me? Was I targeted?

Are you sorry for what happened?

Will you do this to anyone else?

Is my family safe from you?

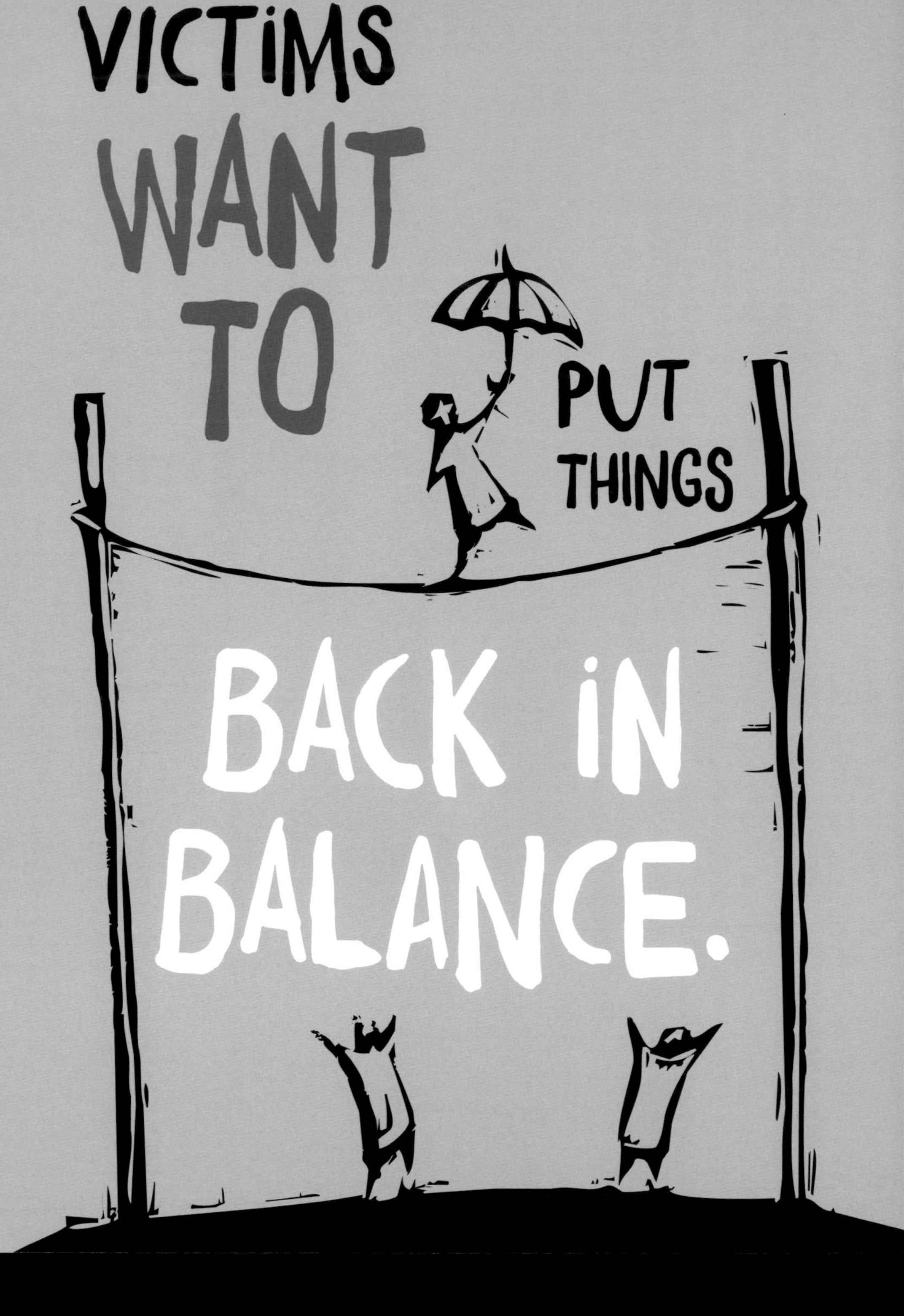
VICTIMS
WANT
TO
PUT
THINGS
BACK IN
BALANCE.

Even offenders who have been sentenced to prison in the regular court system can benefit from restorative justice, and because of it some inmates have changed their lives for the better. Just ask the man who killed Siobhan O'Reilly's dad.

DOES RESTORATIVE JUSTICE ALWAYS WORK?

NO! LIKE ANYTHING ELSE, it's not perfect. In fact, sometimes restorative justice has backfired badly. Take one case in Britain where a victim was encouraged to let an offender visit him in his home to apologize for robbing him. The offender ended up stealing the victim's iPad!

In another case, an angry storekeeper in Australia demanded that a 12-year-old who had shoplifted from him wear a T-shirt printed with the words "I am a thief." The man wanted the shoplifter to feel ashamed of himself, but when local university students decided the T-shirt was cool and started wearing copies of it, the punishment lost its sting.

CHANGING LIVES THROUGH FORGIVENESS

Siobhan O'Reilly was just seven years old when her world changed forever. The family car was being repaired, so her father, Danny, had decided to ride his bike to work in Sonoma, California. As Danny was pedaling home for dinner, a pickup truck, swerving wildly, slammed into him, throwing him from his bike. Danny died there, by the side of the road.

That night, when the police came to tell the O'Reilly family that Danny had been killed by a drunk driver, Siobhan was already in bed. She woke up to the sound of her mother crying. "It was different, going to school afterward," Siobhan remembers. "Kids didn't know how to act toward me, or what to say. So they didn't say anything. And my mom kind of retreated in on herself. It was how she coped."

Two long, lonely years after her father's death, Siobhan asked her mother if she could meet Mike Albertson, the man who had hit and killed her dad, who was now serving a 14-year sentence for his crime. When she learned she was too young to visit him in prison, she did the next best thing: she made Mike a card. It said, "I just wanted to make sure you know that I forgive you. I do still miss my dad; I think that's a lifelong thing. I hope you're feeling OK."

As she read and re-read the card her daughter had made, Patty O'Reilly realized that Siobhan was right. To break free of her hate and anger, Patty needed to talk with the man who had done them so much wrong. Patty visited Mike in jail to deliver the card from Siobhan, and to hear from Mike why he had been driving drunk that night and how he planned to make up for his actions.

"I WANTED TO MAKE SURE YOU KNOW THAT I FORGIVE YOU.

I DO STILL MISS MY DAD; I THINK THAT'S A LIFELONG THING."

The meeting with Mike helped Patty begin to heal from her loss. Then she learned it had helped Mike too, motivating him to join Alcoholics Anonymous and to face the issues in his past that had kept him addicted to drugs and alcohol. Soon, Patty was volunteering in a restorative justice program for prisoners, standing in as a "surrogate victim" when the real victim wasn't willing to take part.

And Siobhan? In the spring of 2015 she turned 18—finally old enough to visit the man she forgave so long ago. Early one May morning, she made the trip to the prison. "I was more nervous and scared than I expected to be," she confessed. "For him to be there in 3-D was over-whelming. I had to go and splash water on my face before we could start.

"He told me what he could remember of the day his truck killed my dad. It was really hard to hear, but I'm glad I got to hear it. I told him how it's been for me since Dad died, and he didn't cry, but he got teary. He thinks about us every day, and he prays for us. I'm grateful to know that the person who caused such dis-ruption in my life feels remorse."

Chapter 4

ON THE ROAD TO RECONCILIATION

SOMETIMES, BEFORE YOU CAN build a future, you need to deal with the past. Young indigenous people around the world are discovering that their journey to reconciliation and healing needs to start by hearing the words "I'm sorry" from their government.

ALICE SPRINGS, AUSTRALIA

Merindeh Yooringun clung to her grandmother Maudie's hand. It was February 13, 2008, and they were in a hurry, hustling as fast as they could to the local community center. Maudie said a man named Kevin Rudd was going to apologize to them. Merindeh was only eight, but she was positive she'd never met anyone called Kevin. And if Kevin was doing the apologizing, why were she and Maudie in such a rush? Surely he would wait until they got there to say he was sorry?

"Maudie, what did Kevin do wrong?"

"Kevin Rudd hasn't done anything, child. It's the ones who came before him who did the harm. Stole the children. That's what Mr. Rudd is saying sorry for."

It seemed to Merindeh as though every Aboriginal family in town was out that day, dressed in their best. Inside the community center, people crowded into a room with a big-screen TV set up in front. Merindeh looked around for the mysterious Kevin, but she saw only the familiar faces of their friends and neighbors.

Abruptly, the TV screen leapt to life, and there was the prime minister of Australia, Kevin Rudd, reading from a piece of paper. "The time has now come for the nation to turn a new page in Australia's history by righting the wrongs of the past," he read. The room got so quiet Merindeh couldn't help hearing what he said.

"We apologize especially for the removal of Aboriginal and Torres Strait Islander children from their families, their communities, and their country," he went on. "For the pain, suffering, and hurt of these Stolen

THEY WANTED US TO FORGET OUR CULTURE, TO FORGET WHAT BEING ABORIGINAL MEANS. IT WAS A TERRIBLE, LONELY WAY TO GROW UP.

Generations, their descendants, and for their families left behind, we say sorry. To the mothers and the fathers, the brothers and the sisters, for the breaking up of families and communities, we say sorry."

Around the room, people were wiping their eyes. Merindeh turned to see Maudie, her tough old granny, blinking back tears. "Maudie, what's wrong?" she asked.

Her grandmother hugged her. "Merindeh, it happened to me—they took me from my family and put me in a mission school. It happened to all my brothers and sisters and cousins, too. They made us talk English, until we forgot our proper language. We weren't allowed to see our parents. They wanted us to forget our culture, to forget what being Aboriginal means. It was a terrible, lonely way to grow up."

Merindeh looked at the serious faces around the room. She knew she would never forget the day her country acknowledged how it had hurt her granny.

HOW TO SAY SORRY... & MEAN IT

An apology like the one Australian Prime Minister Kevin Rudd delivered to the Aboriginal people of Australia is an important first step in reconciliation. Only once governments acknowledge that a group of citizens have been wronged or mistreated is it possible to start healing old wounds and building new relationships based on trust. Most people agree that once governments apologize and accept responsibility for injustices, oppression, or human rights abuses, they should take action to right the wrongs of the past.

In 1995, Queen Elizabeth apologized to the Maori people of New Zealand. It was the first time a British monarch had officially said sorry for anything, and it was long overdue. More than 150 years earlier, in 1840, the British government had signed a treaty with Maori chiefs, promising them rights to the lands and forests of New Zealand and the sea around it in return for giving England the right to rule over the Maori people. The chiefs agreed, but just 20 years later the British broke their promise, stealing 3 million acres of land from the Maori. It took more than a century to right this wrong, but when the queen apologized for the broken treaty, the government of New Zealand returned about 30,000 acres to the Maori, along with millions of dollars in compensation, or **reparations**, to the descendants of those who had been robbed.

In North America, after more than 40 years of pressure, the governments of Canada and the United States finally agreed in 1988 to apologize and pay reparations to people of Japanese descent for the way they were treated during the Second World War. Japanese Canadians and Japanese Americans who were living on the west coast at the start of the war were sent to live in internment camps because the government suspected they might be spies—even though almost all were citizens, and many had never even been to Japan. The governments in both countries seized the property of families who were forced into the camps, and didn't return it at the end of the war. Conditions in the camps were harsh, and many people died or became ill. Families were broken up, and people struggled for years to rebuild their lives after the war. Although the government reparations couldn't make up for their suffering, the money did help to show that the governments' apologies were sincere.

STEREOTYPES VS REALITY

HAVE YOU EVER FELT that an adult judged you unfairly just because you were a kid? Maybe a clerk followed you around a store to make sure you didn't shoplift, or someone shooed you and your friends away from a park, thinking you were up to no good.

That kind of thinking is called stereotyping. It keeps people apart. The people in one group make up their minds about everyone in another group—"they're all crooks" or "they're all liars"—without really getting to know them.

Stereotypes can get passed down from generation to generation, without anyone questioning where the ideas came from. Sometimes bad feelings between groups go back 50, 100, even 1,000 years! These prejudices can be very strong, and they make resolving conflict difficult.

That's where restorative justice can make a difference. When people start to understand one another better, they have a better chance of living together in peace.

THE STOLEN GENERATIONS

Every year on May 26, Australians remember the years of oppression and mistreatment that Aboriginal and Torres Strait Islanders suffered at the hands of the government. It's called National Sorry Day, and it's just one of the ways that indigenous and non-indigenous Australians are trying to **reconcile** after years of racist policies. Until 1967, Aboriginal people didn't even have the right to vote in elections—although their ancestors had been living in Australia for more than 30,000 years!

Many Australians first began questioning the system of laws that discriminated against Aboriginal people thanks to the courage of a young Aboriginal man called Charles Perkins. Charles was born in 1936, in a small town in the center of Australia: Alice Springs. When he was six, the government took Charles away from his mother and sent him to live in an institution for Aboriginal children, to learn English and get a "Christian education."

Charles and the other kids in the school were part of what's now known as Australia's "Stolen Generations." For more than 50 years, tens of thousands of young Aboriginal children were taken from their homes and sent away to schools or orphanages. Growing up away from his family, Charles had one consolation: playing soccer. When he was 14, he and his friends played some boys from the state soccer team. The bare-foot Aboriginal kids beat the older boys, and their coach noticed Charles Perkins. Soon Charles was playing on the state team himself, and while he was still a teenager, he left Australia to play professional soccer in England.

When he came back in 1958, Charles was famous: Australia's first Aboriginal soccer star. Charles decided to use his fame to help Aboriginal

THE GOVERNMENT TOOK CHARLES AWAY AND SENT HIM TO LIVE IN AN INSTITUTION, TO LEARN ENGLISH AND GET A "CHRISTIAN EDUCATION."

Australians gain the same rights as white people. The first step in his plan was to get an education. Charles started studying, and before long he became the first Aboriginal person to go to university.

At university, Charles and some friends formed a group they called Student Action for Aborigines (SAFA). They rented a bus and traveled around the country holding protests against the terrible living conditions Aboriginal people endured, and the discrimination they faced. Thanks to Charles's courage and his group's actions, Australians paid attention for the first time to the living conditions of Aboriginal peoples. They had to face up to the fact that Aboriginal peoples were mistreated and discriminated against. It was the beginning of big changes in Australia.

EVERYONE SWIMS!

ON THE AFTERNOON OF February 19, 1965, a dusty bus pulled up on the outskirts of the little Australian town of Moree. Inside were Charles Perkins, 30 members of Student Action for Aborigines (SAFA), and a few brave, nervous kids from the nearby Aboriginal mission school. They were on their way to the town's pool, to defy the local law that kept Aboriginal people from swimming with whites.

The bus came to a stop outside the pool building, and Charles stepped out. He guided the Aboriginal teens to the entrance, followed by the SAFA members, but the pool staff wouldn't let them in. Charles and the others didn't leave. Instead, they blocked the entrance to the pool, declaring, "If these kids aren't allowed to go through, nobody

goes through." Behind them, the lineup of white townspeople began to mutter angrily. Soon, tempers were rising.

"Imagine. Everybody wanted a swim," Charles recalled years later in an Australian TV documentary. "It was a hot day. So they all gathered and everybody was coming with their towels and everything. 'What's going on?' 'Oh, them bloody blacks are blocking up the entrance here.' 'Get rid of them.' So they called the police. Well, the eggs started flying, stones started flying, then bottles."

The SAFA protest almost started a riot. For three hours the students faced down a crowd of more than 1,000 angry, yelling townspeople and a barrage of food, garbage, and rocks, until finally the pool managers relented and let the students in for a swim.

The face-off was reported in the papers, and people across Australia were embarrassed by the ugly incident. Slowly, laws—and attitudes—in Australia began to change.

Charles Perkins recalled afterward how the courage and companion-ship of his friends on that day helped change his own attitudes toward white Australians: "I began to look at people differently, white people. And I began to understand, you know, white people a bit better and be sort of more open-minded. And I lost a lot of the hate—just sort of drained out of me a bit."

THE TRUTH WILL SET US FREE

For many years, the South African government used the system of **apartheid** (which in the Afrikaans language means "the state of being apart") to deny South African blacks the same rights as white people. Black people couldn't vote, they couldn't travel freely through the country, and they faced restrictions on where they could live and work. There were separate schools, hospitals, and living areas for blacks and whites. The police could arrest black people for nearly any reason—and they often did.

Finally, in 1994, after years of struggle by many brave black activists, apartheid was abolished. Political prisoners, including Nelson Mandela, were released from jail, and the country prepared to hold the first free elections in more than 50 years. That year, Nelson Mandela became the first elected black leader of the country. One of his first decisions was to establish a Truth and Reconciliation Commission that would reveal the truth about what had happened under apartheid. Once everything was out in the open—about killings, beatings, and imprisonments of blacks— Mandela hoped that the people of South Africa could move on. He believed the country had no future until it talked openly about the injustices of the past.

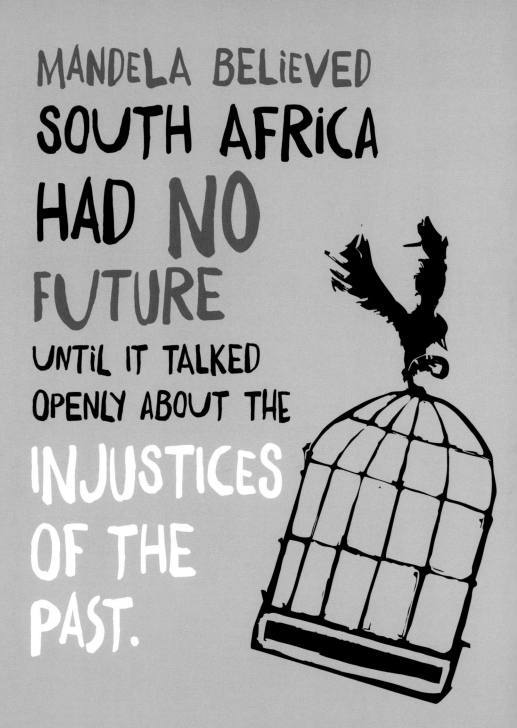

MANDELA BELIEVED
SOUTH AFRICA
HAD NO
FUTURE
UNTIL IT TALKED
OPENLY ABOUT THE
INJUSTICES
OF THE
PAST.

THE CHILDREN'S UPRISING

EARLY ON THE BRIGHT, sunny morning of June 16, 1976, the streets of Soweto, South Africa, were full of kids in school uniforms. But instead of heading for class, these students were walking *away* from their schools. They were taking part in a protest march organized by a local student group against the South African government's policy of teaching all classes in Afrikaans—a language spoken by the white settlers who had colonized South Africa. The black students of Soweto didn't speak Afrikaans, and wanted to be taught in Zulu, or in English. They'd decided to go on strike to show the government they were serious.

That morning, in schools all across Soweto, students put down their pens and filed into the streets. Ten thousand kids began marching toward Orlando Stadium in the center of the city for a peaceful protest gathering. To draw attention to their cause, they carried homemade banners, sang songs, and chanted slogans.

But they never made it to the stadium. Police had blocked the streets the students were planning to march down. When the students reached the barricades, the police threw canisters of tear gas and released attack dogs. The students fought back, throwing rocks and bricks, and that's when an officer gave the command for the police to open fire. More than 200 kids died that day—shot or beaten to death by police.

The Soweto Uprising, as it became known, brought the world's attention to the struggles of black South Africans against the system of apartheid. Now South Africa remembers the uprising each year. June 16 is National Youth Day in South Africa, a day to honor the young people who sacrificed their lives in the fight to create a free and equal country.

THE BITTER TRUTH

The Truth and Reconciliation Commission held hearings in communities all over South Africa, and people who had been involved in the struggle against apartheid came to share their stories. So did people who had worked for the government. For the first time, South African soldiers and police spoke openly about how protesters, activists, and prisoners had been threatened and abused. At last, many black South Africans found out what had happened to their children, parents, or spouses who had disappeared during the apartheid years: how they'd been arrested, tortured, and killed.

The Zulu people of South Africa have a saying: "All truth is bitter." Certainly the truth about apartheid was bitterly hard for the people of South Africa to hear. The hearings were broadcast on national TV, so everyone in the country could watch. No South African could ever again say they didn't know about the abuses black people had suffered.

The process wasn't perfect: the police and soldiers who testified at the Truth and Reconciliation hearings were granted **amnesty** (they were legally pardoned for what they had done), and it made some people angry that the officials responsible for the worst abuses weren't sent to jail. But without the amnesty, the long years of secrecy and lies might never have ended. And the Truth and Reconciliation Commission also gave survivors an opportunity to tell their stories, and to share how their lives and their families' lives had been changed by the violence of apartheid.

Since then, in countries like Ecuador, Guatemala, and El Salvador, truth and reconciliation commissions have helped to bring injustices, oppression, and violence against indigenous people to light. In Canada, members of a commission spent five years criss-crossing the country, gathering testimony from some of the over 150,000 Aboriginal people who as kids were taken away from their families and sent to "residential schools." For more than 100 years, the Canadian government operated these special boarding schools, where Aboriginal children were forced to speak English, and punished if they used their own languages or shared their own cultures or beliefs. The last residential school in Canada wasn't closed until 1996. Almost every Aboriginal family in the country was affected by the mistreatment and abuse that generations of young people suffered in the schools.

As the commission traveled from town to town, hearing the stories of survivors, all of Canada listened as well. Reports were broadcast on TV and radio, videos were shot, and print and online news reporters followed the commission wherever it went. When the Truth and Reconciliation Commission finally released its report in June 2015, Canadians knew

CAN YOU REALLY FIX THE PAST?

NOT EVERYONE AGREES that governments, churches, or other groups should apologize for things that were done a long time ago. Some people argue that you can't apologize for things that were done before you were born, or take responsibility for actions that you didn't commit.

The government of the United States has never issued an official apology for enslaving hundreds of thousands of black people, and some people think it shouldn't—because no Americans are alive today who ever owned a slave. Other people say we all need to take responsibility for the mistakes, violence, and injustices that happened in a country's past.

it was time to make amends for the pain and suffering that Aboriginal people had suffered. The commission made 94 detailed recommendations for ways that Canadians could start to heal the wounds left by the residential school system. Within months, the changes had begun.

Until recently, children haven't been part of truth and reconciliation commissions. That's changing as people learn that kids can use restorative practices in their own lives, and as adults realize how deeply children are affected by violent events.

KIDS IN A STARRING ROLE

In 1996, when a small group of students from Kormilda College in Darwin, Australia, showed up at a big conference on reconciliation, they got a bit of a shock. It turned out that among the hundreds of people at the meeting, they were the only youth. Even at a workshop on "Reconciliation and Youth," the room was entirely filled with adults, all busy discussing what they thought young people wanted.

The students started their own group: Students That Action Reconciliation Seriously, or STARS. They decided the best way to help Aboriginal and non-Aboriginal youth connect with each other was to hold a youth event. Two years later, nearly 300 students from across Australia gathered in Darwin for the National Youth Reconciliation Convention, where every single speech and presentation was delivered by a young person. For some of the non-Aboriginal students, the convention was the first time they had ever met Aboriginal Australians. It was an opportunity for them to hear first-hand about the effects of the Stolen Generations on Aboriginal families.

Chapter 5

HEALING AFTER WAR

FORMER SOUTH AFRICAN PRESIDENT Nelson Mandela once said, "I destroy my enemies when I make them my friends." Restorative justice doesn't usually turn people who have been in conflict with each other into friends, but it can help repair relationships so former enemies can live in peace.

SANTA ELENA, GUATEMALA

"Bring more green paint. We're running out and we still have lots of trees to fill in on this side!"

"Hey, over here! I need some orange for ladies' blouses and blue for the men's pants!"

Twelve-year-old Isabella was on paint duty. It was a tough job, keeping up with all the demands for new colors, fresh brushes, and clean rags, but she loved it. Her youth group had spent several days so far that summer on the giant mural they were painting on the side of the town hall.

"Isabella, get me some yellow and a new brush, quick! I'm going to start on the sun."

Then: "Isabella, we have to start on the bodies now. We'll need lots of red, please."

Isabella walked over to join a group of painters gathered near the center of the long wall. They were looking at an unfinished portion of the painting, where human figures were roughly sketched onto the brownish plaster. Some of the figures pointed guns at others, who were drawn holding out their arms in surrender, or lying sprawled on the ground. More figures were running away, toward the distant green trees at the edge of the mural. Isabella realized that in all the excitement, she had almost forgotten what the painting was about.

Like nearly everyone else in her small hometown of Santa Elena, Isabella was a Mayan, one of the indigenous people of Guatemala. For more than 30 years, starting in 1960, the Guatemalan army had waged a bloody civil war against Mayan rebel groups. Hundreds of thousands of

ISABELLA ALMOST FORGOT THAT THE PAINTING WAS ABOUT THE CIVIL WAR AGAINST THE MAYAN PEOPLE. people disappeared—kidnapped and killed by soldiers acting on the orders of the government. Here, in Isabella's own village, soldiers had killed whole families. The massacre in Santa Elena had happened long before Isabella or her friends were born. Because they were too young to remember the war themselves, the town's children had decided they needed to learn about the violence in their country's past, and they were painting this mural to keep the memory alive. Survivors of the civil war—the kids' parents, grandparents, aunts, and uncles—were sharing their stories so the young people could recreate the scene.

PUTTING THE PIECES BACK TOGETHER

If your country has been torn apart by war, putting the pieces back together can seem almost impossible. Even when the fighting is over, it doesn't always mean that true peace has been achieved—or that the fighting won't start again. Sometimes opposing groups have been enemies for so long, no one can remember a time when there wasn't hatred and violence between them. So how can you build reconciliation between bitter enemies? Some kids are finding ways.

SOMETIMES OPPOSING
GROUPS HAVE BEEN
ENEMIES

FOR SO LONG,

NO ONE

CAN REMEMBER WHEN THERE
WASN'T HATRED AND VIOLENCE.

In Ireland and Israel, in Rwanda and Sri Lanka, young people are working for justice and peace by taking part in discussions and rallies, by writing poetry and songs, by making art and theater, by participating in traditional ceremonies, and by spreading the word about peace on radio programs and through magazines, websites, and social media.

CHILDREN OF WAR

When children are forced to become soldiers, they're victims of war and participants at the same time. Kids like Arn Chorn-Pond of Cambodia know how hard it is to let go of hate and fear when you've been forced to fight, and how important it is to share your story to help make sure violence doesn't happen again.

One evening in 1975, when Arn was eight, his family walked out of their home in Battambang, Cambodia's second-largest city, taking almost nothing with them. They were fleeing from the soldiers of the Khmer Rouge, a military group of radical Communists that was taking over the country. In the chaos, with thousands of people running and trying to hide from the Khmer Rouge, Arn got separated from his family. He never saw his parents or his sister again. The Khmer troops scooped him up, and for the next four years he worked in the rice paddies at a Khmer labor camp, growing food for soldiers. When Arn was 12, the Vietnamese army invaded Cambodia. Vicious fighting broke out between Khmer soldiers and Vietnamese troops, and the Cambodian people were caught in the middle.

Arn remembers the day a Khmer commander handed him a gun and told him that he was a soldier now. He knew that if he refused to fight, he'd be killed. And Arn still dreamed of finding his family. So he agreed, hoping maybe he'd find an opportunity to escape.

The Khmer Rouge trained Arn and other young boys as guerrilla soldiers, sending them out in small groups with instructions to crawl through the jungle, getting as close as they could to the Vietnamese camps. When they were close enough to hear talking, the boys were to shoot, then run for cover in the jungle. Sometimes Arn and the other boys wouldn't know whether they were shooting Vietnamese soldiers or innocent Cambodian villagers. Finally, Arn decided he couldn't go on killing. His only choice was to run away—even though he knew if the Khmer soldiers caught him, he'd be killed. He crept away from the camp one night, taking only his gun and a hammock. For months he wandered alone in the jungle with no idea where he was, surviving on fruit and the occasional fish he was able to catch.

He was near starvation when he at last stumbled across a camp. Arn threw down his gun and walked in with his hands above his head, not knowing whether he was surrendering to the Khmer Rouge or the Vietnamese Army. He was lucky: he'd found his way across the border into Thailand, to a refugee camp filled with others who had fled the violence in Cambodia.

Eventually, an American aid worker succeeded in taking Arn and two other young Cambodians to the United States. Instead of a jungle hut, Arn found himself living in a big, white house in New Hampshire. But life still wasn't easy for Arn. He couldn't speak any English, and he was teased and called names at school. In 1980, the Vietnam War was a recent memory

THEY ALL HAD SOMETHING IN COMMON: WARS HAD STOLEN THEIR FAMILIES, THEIR GOVERNMENTS HAD POISONED THEIR MINDS.

for many Americans, and they were suspicious of anyone with Asian features.

His adoptive father thought Arn could help change people's attitudes if he shared his story. Together, Arn and his father worked on a short speech that he planned to deliver at his family's church. Because Arn still didn't understand much English, he had to memorize all the words. That Sunday, Arn got up to speak in front of the congregation, but before he got very far in his speech, he started crying. Looking around the church, he realized that everyone else, moved by his words, was crying as well.

When he was 16, Arn helped to found an organization called Children of War, which gathered together 42 teenagers who had escaped from war zones all over the world. Their plan was for the teens to travel together throughout the United States, talking to schools and youth groups about wars and violence.

But first they had to get over their distrust of each other. Some of the teenagers in the Children of War group came from countries that had been bitter enemies: on the first day, Arn found himself sitting beside a Vietnamese boy on the bus. Memories of fighting Vietnamese soldiers came flooding back. He remembered his friends who had died on the battlefields in Cambodia. Soon, he and the Vietnamese boy were screaming at each other. Yet by the end of the tour, the kids had realized that although they came from different countries, they all had something in common: wars had stolen their families, and their governments had poisoned their minds against each other. They hugged and cried as they said their goodbyes.

JUSTICE ON THE GRASS

In the past, the dividing lines between people in wars were often actual borders between nations: think about Germany and France, who fought each other in the First and then the Second World Wars. But many conflicts today take place within a single country, between groups of people who follow different religions or belong to different ethnic groups. When people are filled with anger, hatred, and fear—when "us" and "them" thinking gets out of control—they can stop seeing each other as human. When this happens, people become capable of terrible acts, like genocide. One of the bloodiest genocides of the 20th century took place between two groups in the African country of Rwanda.

Rwanda is a small country in east-central Africa. It is about the same size as the state of New Hampshire, and in 1994 just over 8 million people lived there. Most of them were farmers raising crops from Rwanda's fertile soil. On April 6, 1994, a plane carrying the country's president was shot down over the capital city of Kigali. The two main ethnic groups in Rwanda, the Hutus and the Tutsis, each blamed the other for the assassination. Within a few days, anger boiled over, and Hutu armed groups took over Kigali and started massacring Tutsi people. Over the next three months, nearly a million Tutsi people were murdered in Rwanda. Entire villages were wiped out, including children and babies. People who had lived together peacefully for years suddenly killed their neighbors because they were Tutsi.

The genocide ended only when a Tutsi-led armed group, the Rwandan Patriotic Front, took control of the country. Then the Hutu genocidaires (meaning "those who commit genocide") were thrown in prison or fled the country. But Rwanda faced a big problem. How could they bring

RWANDA FACED A BIG PROBLEM. HOW COULD THEY BRING HUNDREDS OF THOUSANDS OF PEOPLE TO JUSTICE?

hundreds of thousands of people to justice? The court system was too slow for the large number of people waiting in jail. So the new Rwandan government decided that the answer was to revive a form of traditional justice—a kind of community restorative justice meeting unique to Rwanda called *gacaca* (pronounced ga-CHA-cha).

Gacaca means "grass" or "hilltop" in the Kinyarwanda language, and the gacaca courts can be translated as "justice on the grass." In the traditional Rwandan justice system, after a crime, the village elders would call a meeting, and together the village would decide what the guilty person should do to make amends. The Rwandan government trained 250,000 people to be gacaca judges, and in 11,000 towns and villages across the country, community members began gathering to hear the confessions of genocidaires. The people who went before a gacaca court weren't the leaders or organizers of the genocide—those individuals have to go before a state court or the International Criminal Tribunal for Rwanda, which was set up by the United Nations. A goal of the gacaca system is to help the community heal, so when genocidaires confess to killing or maiming, they are offered a reduced penalty. Usually, the gacaca judges decide that offenders should help rebuild the community—repairing schools or hospitals, constructing new houses, or working on a local farm. By 2008, the gacaca courts had heard over 100,000 cases in Rwanda.

WHAT IS GENOCIDE?

THE WORD "GENOCIDE" comes from two words meaning "racial killing" (*genos* is the ancient Greek word for race or tribe, and *cide* is from the Latin word for killing). The word was first used in 1944 to describe the deliberate killing of millions of people in Europe by Nazis during the Second World War.

After the war, the United Nations declared genocide a crime under international law, and the Convention on the Punishment and Prevention of the Crime of Genocide came into effect in 1951, with the support of 41 countries. Since then, over 100 more countries have agreed that genocide is a crime against humanity. Sadly, that hasn't meant the end of genocides. In fact, since 1948, there have been at least 20 genocides in countries around the world.

Here's how the United Nations defines genocide: "any of the following acts committed with intent to destroy, in whole or in part, a national, ethnical, racial or religious group, as such:

    ～～ killing members of the group;

    ～～ causing serious bodily or mental harm to members of the group;

    ～～ deliberately inflicting on the group conditions of life calculated to bring about its physical destruction in whole or in part;

    ～～ imposing measures intended to prevent births within the group;

    ～～ forcibly transferring children of the group to another group."

MURDER, MERCY, & FRIENDSHIP

Uzabakiriho Teresphone and Ngirente Phillippe met each other at one of the gacaca hearings. Uzabakiriho is a Hutu. Ngirente is a Tutsi. They'd both been teenagers in the same village at the time of the genocide, and they hadn't seen each other for 13 years. When the violence against

AMAZINGLY, THE YOUNG MAN WAS ABLE TO FORGIVE HIS FATHER'S KILLER.

Tutsis had started, Ngirente's father hid his children at the homes of family friends. Then he tried to take refuge in a banana grove. That's where Uzabakiriho, armed with a machete, found him. Ngirente's father pleaded for mercy, saying he had five children to support. Uzabakiriho told him that if he found the children, he'd kill them. Then he cut off the older man's head.

Ngirente and his sisters were devastated to find out their father had been killed, but they managed to survive the genocide. Afterward, Ngirente went to university and studied law. When the gacaca courts opened, he volunteered to work at the one in his community. He helped to prepare the genocidaires for their trials, encouraging them to tell their stories openly and to ask for forgiveness from the people they had harmed. But when Uzabakiriho described in the gacaca court how he had killed Ngirente's father, Ngirente didn't know how he would be able to overcome his anger and welcome Uzabakiriho back into the community.

Uzabakiriho was terrified when he learned that the son of the man he had killed was at the trial. After the genocide he had fled the country, but he came back to Rwanda and turned himself in. He had already spent several years in prison when his turn came to tell his story at the gacaca hearing. Like many genocidaires, Uzabakiriho worried that people might try to take revenge on him when they learned what he had done. So when Ngirente approached Uzabakiriho after the trial and invited him to come to his house to meet his wife and family, Uzabakiriho wondered if he would be walking into a trap.

Getting to know Uzabakiriho was the only way Ngirente could imagine coming to terms with what had happened to his father. Finally, months after the trial, Uzabakiriho accepted Ngirente's invitation. He brought food and wine, and he asked Ngirente and his wife to forgive him. Amazingly, Ngirente was able to forgive his father's killer, and the two young men are now friends and colleagues.

OVERCOMING A HISTORY OF HATE

In Northern Ireland, a bitter conflict between two religious groups has been going on for hundreds of years. Protestants and Catholics have been fighting one another for control of the country since the 1600s, when the English army occupied Ireland. Irish Catholics resented being ruled by English Protestants and wanted Ireland to be a separate and independent country. In the middle of the 20th century, this disagreement grew violent. Extremists on both sides armed themselves, forming paramilitary groups (groups of ordinary citizens who organize themselves as small armies). The groups fought each other in the streets, and the Catholics fought against the British soldiers who were there to keep the peace and enforce British rule.

SHOOTINGS, BOMBINGS, KIDNAPPINGS, BEATINGS, AND INTIMIDATION

HAPPENED REGULARLY. MANY PEOPLE WERE AFRAID TO LEAVE THEIR HOMES AT NIGHT.

From the 1960s until the 1990s, Northern Ireland was a dangerous place. Shootings, bombings, kidnappings, beatings, and intimidation happened regularly. Many people were afraid to leave their homes at night, Catholics were afraid to venture down Protestant streets, and Protestants didn't dare shop in Catholic stores. Thousands of innocent people died. The Irish call these dark times "the Troubles."

Today, the Troubles are over. A peace accord called the Good Friday Agreement was signed in 1997. But Northern Ireland is still a divided society. Catholics and Protestants live in their own neighborhoods and go to their own shops and schools.

In 2011, a group of kids in the town of Monaghan decided that young Catholics and Protestants could be friends if they could just meet each other. But there was nowhere for young people to hang out, except at school—and there were separate schools for Protestants and Catholics. They needed a place of their own, and they needed to convince the local government to help them build it. Reasoning that the government couldn't ignore all the kids in town, they organized a survey to find out what kids thought—could Catholics and Protestants get along in a shared space? They convinced teachers to hand out the survey in classes, posted it on Facebook and Tumblr, and stood on street corners asking kids to fill it out. Eventually, they got more than 1,000 kids to participate.

The results? While almost everyone who completed the survey said religion wasn't important to them when they were choosing friends, only a small number knew anyone of another religion. And everyone agreed the town needed somewhere for young people to meet one another and make friends. The kids were right: the government didn't ignore them.

Soon the Monaghan Peace Café was set up—a casual spot where teens of both religions could hang out, chat, make new friends—and begin to break down the barriers between Catholics and Protestants.

STOPPING VIOLENCE WITH SOCCER

IN THE SMALL, crowded, war-torn country of Palestine, finding some-place safe to play soccer can be a challenge. And until recently it was even harder if you were a girl, because there were no girls' soccer leagues. Liza Musleh helped to change that by starting one of her country's first all-girls soccer teams in 2004.

Seeing how attitudes toward girls in sport could change led her to start thinking about other changes she wanted to see, such as peace between her country and Israel.

In 2008, Liza joined an unusual mixed soccer team. Half of the players were boys and half were girls; half were Palestinian and half were Israeli. The team practiced in Israel, and to get there Liza and the other Palestinian players had to wake up at the crack of dawn, make their way through army checkpoints, and cross the border into Israel. But it was worth it. They were training to compete against kids from around the world at the Football for Hope Festival—part of the 2010 FIFA world cup in South Africa.

Liza's team had a lot of obstacles to overcome. The players didn't all speak the same language. Boys and girls hadn't played together before. They didn't even know if they could trust the players from the other country. But slowly, as they drilled and practiced their moves, they learned to open up to each other. By the time the kids went to South Africa, they were truly a team. They didn't win the competition, but they felt like they'd scored a victory just by playing together: soccer had helped them to overcome prejudice, fear, and a long history of violence.

In 2011, Liza was nominated for the International Children's Peace Prize for her efforts to spread peace and equality through sports.

CREATING PEACE IN COLOMBIA

In Colombia, young activists like Mayerly Sanchez have been working for years to create peace.

Mayerly is one of the leaders of the Children's Movement for Peace, which she and her friends started when they were only 14 years old. Their club started out small: the kids met in a local park, where they wrote and performed their own plays about peace and tolerance. It was hard to convince other kids to join the club at first. Drug dealers, gang violence, and civil war were part of life in Colombia, and people were afraid to speak out. Mayerly remembers feeling frustrated, and overwhelmed. "If a kid's mother is murdered, how do you talk to him about peace?"

In 1996, Mayerly was invited to a national conference sponsored by UNICEF, where she met other young peace activists from all over Colombia. At the conference, Mayerly and the others dreamed big: what if Colombia held a national Children's Vote for Peace? It would be a chance for kids to tell the adults in Colombia that they wanted the violence in their neighborhoods to stop.

Less than a year later, the Children's Vote took place, and 3 million kids from every town and city in Colombia went to the polls to vote for peace. Ahead of the vote, Mayerly and her friends wrote to all the gangs they could, asking them to put down their guns for one day and let children walk to the vote in peace. And they did. It was the first day without violence in Colombia in more than 40 years.

Almost 100,000 kids have joined the Movement for Peace, and more sign up every month. The members are always looking for new ways to end violence and bring peace into their lives and their communities.

Chapter 6

CREATING HOPE FOR THE FUTURE

THE FIRST STEP on the restorative justice journey is making sure that everyone's voice is heard—even those who no longer have a voice.

GULU DISTRICT, NORTHERN UGANDA

From the corner of his eye, Daniel caught sight of a collection of small huts in the distance. He swerved his bicycle off the road and onto a narrow, muddy track leading toward the tiny settlement. When he arrived in the center of the village, curious eyes looked out at him from the doorways of family compounds, but no one came to greet him. Daniel wasn't surprised at the cool reception—this was northern Uganda, where after years of violent terrorism, villagers were wary of strangers. Even harmless-looking teenagers on muddy bicycles might not be safe to trust.

Daniel leaned his bike carefully against an acacia tree, took a clipboard from his bag, and uncapped a pen. He walked purposefully toward the nearest of the small earthen-walled houses and rapped on the wooden door. A woman with a baby in her arms peeked out at him but didn't speak. Daniel cleared his throat.

"Good morning, *Nyabo*," he said in the Luganda language, using the polite term for an older woman. "How are you today? My name is Daniel Okella Kitara, and I am from Children as Peacemakers. We're doing a survey to discover how many children have died or gone missing in the war against the Lord's Resistance Army. May I please ask you some questions?"

"What do you wish to know?" she said quietly.

"Nyabo, I need to know, have any children from this house died or gone missing in the war?"

There was a long pause. "Yes," said the woman in a low voice. "Two children are missing. My baby's big brother and sister. Soldiers stole them from us five years ago. I haven't seen my children since."

Daniel noted down the children's names, their ages when they disappeared, and how and when they were kidnapped. Then he asked, "Nyabo, if you wish to tell me anything about your children, I will write it down. We are doing this survey because Uganda must never forget how many children suffered in this war."

Tears ran down the woman's face, but she smiled as she answered. "Oh, my son was a funny one. He always had a joke, and he loved to make us laugh. I called my daughter 'little bird' because she sang every morning."

Before he left to visit the next home in the village, Daniel thanked her for speaking to him. "Nyabo, we are planning to create a memorial to the lost children in the middle of the town square in Gulu. When it is built I hope you will come and see it." As he walked away, he realized what made this village, and the others he had visited for the survey, so unusual: there was no laughter, and no singing. They were gone, along with the missing children.

THERE WAS NO LAUGHTER IN THE VILLAGE, NO SINGING— THE CHILDREN WERE MISSING.

IN THEIR NAME

THE SURVEY BY THE YOUNG RESEARCHERS of the Children as Peacemakers group proved that children were the most deeply hurt of all Ugandans by the years of violence caused by the Lord's Resistance Army, or LRA, a vicious terrorist group. For 20 years, from 1986 until 2006, the LRA, led by a man called Joseph Kony, burned villages and farms, and murdered, injured, and terrorized people across Uganda. When they needed more fighters, the LRA kidnapped children and forced them to become rebel soldiers: more than 66,000 Ugandan kids were stolen from their families by the LRA. They were tortured, drugged, and made to fight or to work as slaves. Many died—from violence, disease, starvation, or neglect.

In the area around the small city of Gulu, 10,372 people died or disappeared during the war. Out of every 10 of those vanished people, 7 were kids or teenagers under 18. Thousands more young people lost their homes and family members, went hungry, and had to live with the constant fear of being kidnapped. Are there any young people in Gulu whose lives haven't been affected by the LRA's violence? Probably not.

But the Ugandan survey also proved that young people are resilient—they can bounce back. Many of the surveyors who bicycled from compound to compound to collect the names of the dead and disappeared had been kidnapped themselves, or had been forced to flee to refugee camps during the war. Yet they came back to their communities and decided to work for peace.

REDISCOVERING THE PAST

Many young people today are working to recover and honor their culture's history. That means making sure that the memories of how people resisted and suffered in wars and conflicts aren't forgotten or glossed over. It can also mean reconnecting with elders to learn about cultural traditions that have been almost lost to young people.

On Canada's Pacific coast, First Nations youth in the Heiltsuk community are helping to revive their culture's traditional justice practices. In earlier times, when a member of a Heiltsuk community hurt someone or committed a crime, the elders held a healing circle and looked for ways to bring the community back into balance. Sometimes, they banished the offender from the community for a time.

By the 1950s, the Heiltsuk were forced to give up their traditions and accept white Canadian justice: police, judges, prisons. Then, in 1979, a judge allowed the Heiltsuk to decide how to help a troubled young man from the town of Bella Bella, British Columbia.

Frank Brown was a 15-year-old Heiltsuk who had been convicted of a serious robbery and beating. He was headed for jail, but then some elders from his community asked for a chance to help Frank through traditional justice. The judge accepted their proposal. Not long afterward, at a Heiltsuk healing circle, the elders explained to Frank that if he wanted to be accepted back into their community, he would first have to spend eight months alone in the bush, banished on a remote island.

Community members checked in on Frank occasionally, to bring food and make sure he was coping with his isolation. But mostly Frank had to fend for himself—by hunting, building his own shelter, and relying on

TO BE
ACCEPTED BACK,
FRANK WOULD
HAVE TO SPEND
EIGHT MONTHS
ALONE IN THE
BUSH.

his instincts and traditional skills. The experience changed Frank. After his banishment, he finished high school and went on to college. In 1986, Frank led an expedition of Heiltsuk paddlers in traditional canoes 300 kilometers (about 200 miles) down the coast to Vancouver. That journey helped revive the Heiltsuk people's pride in their history as ocean-going paddlers. A year later, Frank started the Heiltsuk Rediscovery Project to help young people in Bella Bella learn traditional skills and stay out of trouble with the law.

SOLVE THIS!

Humans have developed an incredible number of ways to deal with conflict, apply justice, and make peace with each other. And we're always coming up with new methods to show that we want to reconcile. But some of the challenges we face today aren't necessarily conflicts between groups of people.

For instance, what about conflicts between people and corporations? Imagine a giant multinational drug company that sends its employees to investigate a remote tribe's natural remedy for an illness. The drug company's scientists discover that the remedy is effective, and the company patents the drug and markets it. They make millions, but don't pay anything to the indigenous people. Not many people would consider this fair, but it's a common practice, and there are no laws to stop it.

CAN RESTORATIVE JUSTICE BE ADAPTED TO GET CORPORATIONS TO MAKE AMENDS?

Other practices aren't against the law, either, but lots of people now agree those activities are hurting people, animals, and the planet: things like clear-cut logging, damming rivers, destructive fishing practices, oil spills that destroy environments, and toxic runoff from mines and industrial plants that poisons lakes and wildlife. It can be tough to hold big industrial polluters accountable, but can restorative justice be adapted to get corporations to make amends?

The challenge now, on a global scale, is to bring our world back into balance. Part of the answer may lie in helping opposing groups see that they both have an interest in finding solutions to the world's environmental problems.

ECO JUSTICE FOR THE WAIKATO RIVER

In 2011, the city of Hamilton, New Zealand, spilled 90,000 liters of human waste into the Waikato River. That's about 24,000 gallons of urine and feces—enough to fill a good-sized swimming pool. The state government could have made the city pay a fine of up to $600,000 for polluting the river, but a group of local environmentalists didn't see how that would help the dirty Waikato. So they came up with a novel suggestion.

Instead of a trial, they asked the government to hold a restorative justice conferencing circle. But how could the victim—the Waikato River—take part? The environmentalists had a creative solution. The president

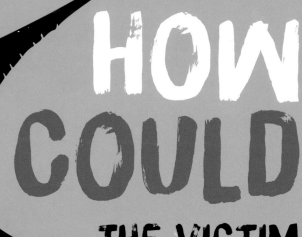

HOW COULD

THE VICTIM—
THE
WAIKATO
RIVER—

TAKE
PART IN
THE TRIAL?

of the Waikato River Enhancement Society "became" the river at the circle, explaining to the others how badly it had been affected by the city's negligence. City council members took the offenders' role, since it was part of their job to make sure the city's waste was properly treated.

The river-victim and the city-offenders worked out a plan to clean the river and to help restore it to a more natural state. They agreed that the city would plant trees and native plants along the riverbanks as compensation for the harm done.

The case got other environmentalists thinking about how to use restorative justice to fight for the rights of nonhuman victims. And what about victims who haven't been born yet? Some environmental crimes, such as nuclear disasters, affect people for generations. Who can speak for the children to come? These are issues restorative justice experts are grappling with today.

COURAGE ON BLOODY FRIDAY

EVERY YEAR, one member of the City of Belfast Youth Orchestra in Ireland receives the Stephen Parker Memorial Prize. It's an unusual award. It doesn't go to the best player in the orchestra; in fact, it doesn't really matter if the winner is a talented musician or not. Instead, the prize is given to someone who "tried very hard."

Stephen Parker tried very hard, and his family wanted to honor that when they set up the prize in his memory. He tried hard in his music and he died while trying his best to save others.

continued on page 118

continued from page 117

In 1972, Stephen was 14, and he had his first summer job, working as a delivery boy for a small grocery shop near his home in Belfast. One Friday afternoon in July he was standing in the sunshine outside the shop when he noticed something odd. A car drove up, screeched to a stop in front of the grocery, and the driver got out of the car and ran off without bothering to lock the car door behind him. This was during Ireland's Troubles, when violence was common in the city. Stephen was suspicious. He stepped forward to take a closer look at the car and saw a large, lumpy shape on the back seat. Stephen realized he was looking at a bomb.

Stephen could have run away, but instead he waved his arms and shouted to get people's attention: "I think that's a dangerous car!" Seconds later, the bomb exploded. The explosion ripped apart the grocery shop, injuring dozens of people, and killing Stephen Parker. It was just one of 27 bombs that were set off by the Irish Republican Army (a group fighting for an independent Ireland and the removal of British soldiers) that day. Hundreds of people were injured or killed. July 21, 1972, is now known as Bloody Friday in Ireland, and it's remembered as one of the most violent days in the country's history.

Stephen came from a family of peace activists. His parents decided to create a prize in his name to make sure the memory of his courageous action lived on, encouraging others to keep on trying—through music, and working for a peaceful future in Ireland.

A HEALING JOURNEY

SOMETIMES, SOMETIMES JUSTICE can't be done. Often, victims of crime or war or oppression will never know the people who hurt them. No one will ever look them in the eye and say, "I'm sorry." What happens then?

WHILE I WAS WRITING THIS BOOK, I was the victim of a crime. Luckily it wasn't a big crime and no one was hurt, but it made me think in new ways about justice. Here's what happened: one night I walked out of my local library, my mind buzzing from all the stories about crime and justice I'd been reading. I was ready to jump on my bike and pedal home, but something about my bicycle looked...different. It took my brain a second or two to process what I was seeing: my handlebars were missing!

When I looked more closely, I realized that not only had my handlebars been stolen, but so had my brakes. I was spitting mad. Without brakes and handlebars, my bike was useless. How dare some thief take away my favorite way of getting around?

The repairs were expensive and took several days, and afterward I didn't feel safe leaving the bike outside the public library again. When I wanted to go to the library, I took the bus. I missed riding my bike, and I usually spent the trip thinking angrily that if it hadn't been for the thief, I'd be happily zooming down the streets on my bike instead of cooped up on a stuffy bus.

And I had questions—lots of them.

"Why did you pick my bike?"

"What did you do with the parts? Did you sell them, or was taking them just some cruel joke?"

"Have you done this before?"

"Are you going to do it again?"

I'm lucky to live in a city and a country that is safe for most people. I don't have to worry about being shot or assaulted on the streets when I go out. But the library is near an area of my city where a large number of homeless, mentally ill, and drug-addicted people live—and their lives are much more difficult and dangerous than mine. As I thought more about the theft, I started to wonder what "my" thief's life was like. Was he or she homeless? Were my bike parts sold for money for food—or to buy drugs?

WERE MY BIKE PARTS SOLD FOR MONEY FOR FOOD— OR TO BUY DRUGS?

What I needed was a restorative justice meeting with the thief. But the police haven't caught the person who stole my bike parts. And it's not likely they will. In fact, according to the FBI, less than 20 percent of crimes result in an arrest. Even if the police arrested someone for the theft, there's no guarantee the offender would agree to meet with me. Although 9 out of 10 people who are arrested and go to trial for a crime eventually plead guilty, meeting with a victim to say "I'm sorry for what I did to you" is much harder than standing in court while a lawyer reads out your guilty plea. I knew it was unlikely I'd ever get the answers to my questions. I'll never meet the person who robbed me.

So I wondered, can restorative justice happen without the offender? From talking with Siobhan O'Reilly in California, I knew that it could be successful for offenders even when the victims didn't want to participate. Could it work the other way as well? It turns out that in some cases, it can. Lorenn Walker is a lawyer in Hawaii, and she's been building a program to help victims of crime in cases where the offender isn't known or won't agree to participate. Lorenn isn't only a lawyer: she's also been an offender (she went to jail when she was just 16) and the victim of a crime (she was assaulted when she was 24, and the man who hurt her was never caught). So she realizes how tough it is for offenders to admit they're responsible for hurting someone, and she also knows how hard it is to live with unanswered questions and the fear and anger that victims of crime feel. The program she developed is very simple, but it can help people who have been harmed to move on with their lives after a crime.

Lorenn organizes small group meetings called "restorative conversations." In the meetings, people who have been victims of a crime tell their stories and share how they are feeling. Then together the group decides on something each victim can do to help that person to heal. That might mean helping out in their community—like volunteering for an organization that helps street kids—to fight conditions that cause crime. Most people who participate say they feel better afterward about what happened to them. There's still a big piece missing—justice for the person who hurt them. But restorative conversations help victims to accept that even though they'll likely never hear the words "I'm sorry," they can still heal, and sometimes they can even say, "I forgive you."

> EVEN THOUGH THEY'LL NEVER HEAR THE WORDS "I'M SORRY," THEY CAN STILL HEAL.

It sounded great, but I was long way from Hawaii. I thought and thought as I continued reading about restorative justice. What would help me feel safe enough to bring my bike back to the library? Eventually I decided I needed to trust the people in my city again, so I got back on my bike. And for each bike ride I took to the library while I finished this book, I put the money I would have spent on bus fare aside. When the book was finished, I sent the money to an organization that advocates for justice for homeless people in my city.

Learning about restorative justice has shown me that sometimes conflicts can actually create opportunities for us to make the world a better

SOMETIMES CONFLICTS CAN ACTUALLY CREATE OPPORTUNITIES FOR US TO MAKE THE WORLD A BETTER PLACE.

place. By understanding the deeper reasons behind crimes, we can make changes to our societies—and ourselves—that can go a long way toward preventing violence and crime from happening in the future. We won't make our cities safer to live in by building more prisons: instead, we need to build more caring communities.

Restorative justice isn't going to change the world overnight. It won't end all crime or prevent all wars. But it's a powerful way to change people's attitudes and to start building a more peaceful society. And it is just one of the many ways that people, young and old, are working to help change our world for the better. Brave, dedicated people in every country on earth are fighting against poverty and racism; building schools and training teachers so all kids have the chance to get a good education; making sure that everyone has access to clean water and healthy food; working for equality for girls and women; standing up to unjust governments; and spreading the word about peace, freedom, and justice. There's still a long way to go—but with so many inspiring examples, you're sure to find a way to join in and help change the world. Whether you start in your school, your neighborhood, or even your own home, why not ask yourself, "What can I do to help build peace and understanding between people?"

As I was writing the last few pages of this book, I continued to bike to the library. One night, I noticed there was again something different about my bike. This time, someone had left a red rose on the seat. I like to think it was from the thief—making things right.

GLOSSARY

amnesty: a government pardon to a group of people who have broken the law but have not yet been convicted

amygdala: a small, almond-shaped cluster of cells in the brain, thought to control emotions and decision-making

anthropologist: someone who studies human culture, past and present

anti-Semitism: hatred or prejudice against Jewish people

apartheid: a South African government system that separated people by race, in place from 1948 to 1994

charge: a specific crime a person has been accused of committing

corporal punishment: punishment that is applied to the body, such as spanking, whipping, or caning

court: a place where justice is administered

crime: an act that breaks a law

criminal law: law that sets forth how the state deals with crime

criminologist: someone who studies crime, its causes, and its effects on society

empathy: the ability to understand what another person is experiencing, from their point of view

evidence: information presented during a trial that is used to persuade a judge or jury

felony: a serious crime

judge: a government official who runs court proceedings, with the authority to decide whether someone accused of a crime is innocent or guilty

jury: a group of citizens who are selected to listen to evidence in court and decide whether the accused is innocent or guilty

misdemeanor: a minor crime

neuroscientist: a scientist who studies the nervous system, particularly the brain and how it affects human behavior

offender: someone who has been convicted of breaking the law, or who has pleaded guilty to breaking the law

plea: a statement an accused person makes in court when asked if they are "guilty" or "not guilty" of a crime

primatologist: a scientist who studies nonhuman primates, such as chimpanzees

probation: a situation where an offender is supervised and must follow certain conditions

probation officer: a person who supervises offenders and supports them after they are released from prison

prosecutor: a lawyer who argues in court against a person who has been charged with a crime

public defender/ defense counsel: a lawyer who represents a person charged with a crime

reconciliation: bringing people or groups together to restore peaceful relations after a conflict

rehabilitate: to improve a person's behavior so they won't commit further criminal acts

reparation: money or other aid given to make amends to people or groups who have been wronged

restorative justice: a system of justice that focuses on repairing the harm done by an offense and rehabilitating the offender

retributive justice: a system of justice in which offenders are punished for crimes

sentence: the punishment ordered by a court for a offender convicted of a crime

stereotype: a belief that a group of people are all alike in some way

testify: to give information about a crime in court

trial: a hearing that takes place in court, where parties present the case for or against someone accused of a crime, and a judge or jury decides whether the person is guilty or innocent

victim: a person who has been harmed by a crime

witness: a person called upon by either side in court to give information about a crime

SELECTED SOURCES

Assembly of First Nations. "Fact Sheet: Quality of Life of First Nations, June 2011." Retrieved September 11, 2015. afn.ca/uploads/files/factsheets/quality_of_life_final_fe.pdf

Bloomfield, David, Teresa Barnes, and Luc Huyse (eds). *Reconciliation after Violent Conflict: A Handbook*. Stockholm, Sweden: International Institute for Democracy and Electoral Assistance, 2003.

"Charles Perkins." Australian Biography series. Film Australia. 1998. Retrieved August 27, 2015. australianbiography.gov.au/subjects/perkins.

Conflict, Culture, and Memory Lab. University of Waterloo. ccmlab.uwaterloo.ca/index.html.

Cooley, Dennis. *From Restorative Justice to Transformative Justice*. Ottawa: Law Commission of Canada, 2007.

de Waal, Frans B. M. "Primates—A Natural Heritage of Conflict Resolution." *Science* 289, no. 5479 (July 28, 2000): 586–90.

——.*Peacemaking among Primates*. Cambridge, MA: Harvard University Press, 1989.

Diamond, Jared. *The World Until Yesterday: What Can We Learn from Traditional Societies?* New York: Penguin Books, 2012.

Dickson-Gilmore, Jane and Carol La Prairie. *Will the Circle Be Unbroken: Aboriginal Communities, Restorative Justice, and the Challenges of Conflict and Change*. Toronto: University of Toronto Press, 2005.

Elliot, Heather, ed. *Children and Peacebuilding: Experiences and Perspectives*. Australia: World Vision, 2002.

Feinstein, Clare and Claire O'Kane. *Adult's War and Young Generation's Peace: Children's Participation in Armed Conflict, Post Conflict and Peace Building*. Save the Children Norway, 2008.

——.*I Painted Peace: Handbook on Peace Building with and for Children and Young People*. Save the Children Norway, 2008.

Fisanick, Christina. *The Rwandan Genocide*. Farmington Hills, MI: Greenhaven Press, 2004.

Frey, Rebecca Joyce. *Genocide and International Justice*. New York: Infobase Publishing, 2009.

Galinsky, Ellen. *Youth and Violence: Students Speak Out for a More Civil Society*. New York: Families and Work Institute, 2002.

Gardner, Trevor. *Make Students Part of the Solution, Not the Problem. Phi Delta Kappan* 96, no. 2 (October 2014) 8–12. doi: 10.1177/0031721714553403.

Green, Ross Gordon and Kearney F. Healy. *Tough on Kids: Rethinking Approaches to Youth Justice.* Saskatoon, SK: Purich Publishing, 2003.

"How a Drunken Rampage Changed Legal History." *Ottawa Citizen,* March 2, 2007, originally published September 11, 2004. www.canada.com/story.html?id=68c9484e-7dfa-41a6-976a-fcd9b0a96424.

Human Rights Watch. *Lasting Wounds: Consequences of Genocide and War on Rwanda's Children.* New York: Human Rights Watch, 2003.

Hurlbert, Margot A (ed). *Pursuing Justice: An Introduction to Justice Studies.* Halifax, NS: Fernwood Publishing, 2011.

Jones, Tricia S. and Randy Compton, eds. *Kids Working It Out: Stories and Strategies for Making Peace in Our Schools.* San Francisco: Jossey-Bass, 2003.

Kelly, Russ. *From Scoundrel to Scholar...the Russ Kelly Story.* Fergus, Ont: R. Kelly Pub., 2006.

Liebmann, Marian. *Restorative Justice: How It Works.* London: Jessica Kingsley Publishers, 2007.

Llewellyn, Jennifer J. and Robert Howse. *Restorative Justice: A Conceptual Framework.* Ottawa: Law Commission of Canada, 1998.

"LRT Homicide Victim Once Ran Innovative Youth Program." *CBC News.* February 6, 2012. cbc.ca/news/canada/edmonton/lrt-homicide-victim-once-ran-innovative-youth-program-1.1171332.

Miethe, Terance D. and Hong Lu. *Punishment: A Comparative Historical Perspective.* Cambridge, UK: Cambridge University Press, 2005.

Monture-Okanee, Patricia. "Thinking about Aboriginal Justice: Myths and Revolution." In *Continuing Poundmaker and Riel's Quest: Presentations Made at a Conference on Aboriginal Peoples and Justice.* Saskatoon, SK: Purich Publishing, 1993.

Morris, Ruth. *Stories of Transformative Justice.* Toronto: Canadian Scholars Press, 2000.

Morrison, Brenda. *Restoring Safe School Communities: A Whole School Response to Bullying, Violence and Alienation.* Annandale, NSW: The Federation Press, 2007.

Patel, Eboo. *Acts of Faith: The Story of an American Muslim, the Struggle for the Soul of a Generation.* Boston: Beacon Press, 2010.

Perry, John, ed. *Repairing Communities through Restorative Justice.* Lanham, MD: American Correctional Association, 2002.

"Really, Really Sorry." *The Economist* vol. 368, no. 8335 (August 2, 2003): 54.

Reisel, Daniel. The Neuroscience of Restorative Justice. Ted Talks: 2012. youtube.com/watch?v=tzJYY2p0QIc.

Reyes, Alejandro. "Rough Justice: A Caning in Singapore Stirs up a Fierce Debate about Crime and Punishment." *Asiaweek*. May 25, 1994. Accessed online. corpun. com/awfay9405.htm.

Roht-Arriaza, Naomi and Javier Mariezcurrena (eds). *Transitional Justice in the Twenty-First Century: Beyond Truth versus Justice*. Cambridge, UK: Cambridge University Press, 2006.

Rosenberg, R. S., S. L. Baughman, and J. N. Bailenson. *Virtual Superheroes: Using Superpowers in Virtual Reality to Encourage Prosocial Behavior*. PLoS ONE 8, no.1 (2013). doi: 10.1371/journal.pone.0055003.

Ross, Rupert. *Returning to the Teachings: Exploring Aboriginal Justice*. Toronto: Penguin Books, 1996.

Royko, Mike. "Readers Get 'Behind' Flogging of Vandal." *New York Daily News*. March 30, 1994. s88.photobucket.com/user/corpuncom/media/archive/3658a.jpg.html

Sandel, Michael J. *Justice: What's the Right Thing To Do?* New York: Farrar, Straus and Giroux, 2009.

Schnabel, Albrecht and Anara Tabyshalieva. *Escaping Victimhood: Children, Youth and Post-Conflict Peacebuilding*. United Nations University Press: New York, 2013.

"So Not Sorry." *Maclean's,* April 5, 2012.

"Teenage Perspectives 2011." Youth Work Ireland—Monaghan. youthworkireland.ie/monaghan/wp-content/uploads/2011/06/teenage_perspectives_report2011.pdf.

Walker, Lorenn. *Restorative Justice without Offender Participation: A Pilot Program for Victims*. Restorative Practices E-Forum, 2004. Accessed at Social Science Research Network: ssrn.com/abstract=2139140.

Westervelt, Eric. "An Alternative to Suspension and Expulsion: 'Circle Up!'" National Public Radio. December 17, 2014. npr.org/blogs/ed/2014/12/17/347383068/an-alternative-to-suspension-and-expulsion-circle-up?sc=tw.

Zehr, Howard. *Changing Lenses: A New Focus for Crime and Justice*. Scottdale, PA: Herald Press, 1995. emu.edu/now/restorative-justice/2011/03/10/restorative-or-transformative-justice/.

——. "Restorative or Transformative Justice?" *Restorative Justice Blog*. March 10, 2011. Retrieved March 3, 2013. emu.edu/now/restorative-justice/2011/03/10/restorative-or-transformative-justice

INDEX

ACKNOWLEDGMENTS

MANY PEOPLE CONTRIBUTED to the making of this book. I am very grateful to Russ Kelly and Siobhan O'Reilly for telling me their stories and answering my questions with such openness and honesty. Taylor-Rae Foster at the Youth Restorative Action Project in Edmonton generously shared her memories of her former colleague, Heather Thurier. Liza Musleh patiently responded to all my emails, filling me in on details of her life as a soccer-loving girl in Palestine. Frank Tester of the Vancouver Association for Restorative Justice gave me good advice and suggestions for research that helped to shape the book. Thanks to Rachel Perkins for permission to quote from the 1999 Australian Biography documentary of her father, Charlie Perkins. And, for their patience, good humor, and keen, intelligent editing, I am enormously indebted to Barbara Pulling, Elizabeth McLean, Paula Ayer, and Colleen MacMillan.

ABOUT THE AUTHOR

MARILEE PETERS remembers a day not so long ago when thousands of people in her city turned out in the pouring rain to show their support for Canada's Truth and Reconciliation movement. A sea of multicolored umbrellas mingled with Aboriginal capes, and the sounds of drumming, chanting, and cheering filled the streets. So when the opportunity came along to write about restorative justice and reconciliation, she jumped at the chance to learn more about how it has helped heal relationships and change lives all around the world.

Marilee is also the author of *Patient Zero: Solving the Mysteries of Deadly Epidemics* and *10 Rivers That Shaped the World*. She lives with her husband and two children in rainy but awesome Vancouver, British Columbia.